The New Tax Guide for Artists of Every Persuasion

The New Tax Guide for Artists of Every Persuasion

**Actors, Directors, Musicians, Singers
and Other Show Biz Folk
Visual Artists and Writers**

PETER JASON RILEY, CPA

LIMELIGHT EDITIONS
New York

First Limelight Edition, January 2002

Manufactured in the United States of America.

Library of Congress Cataloging-in-Publication Data

Riley, Peter Jason.
    The new tax guide for artists of every persuasion : actors, directors, musicians, singers, and other show biz folk visual artists and writers / Peter Jason Riley.— 1st ed.
        p. cm.
    ISBN 0-87910-966-1
    1. Artists—Taxation—Law and legislation—United States. 2. Entertainers—Taxation—Law and legislation—United States. 3. Theatrical producers and directors—Taxation—Law and legislation—United States. I. Title.

    KF6369.8.A7 R55 2002
    343.7305'2'0247—dc21

                          2001050736

Designed by Mulberry Tree Press, Inc. (www.mulberrytreepress.com)

Thanks to:

- ✓ My lovely wife Ruth who puts up with my endless discussions and ruminations on taxes and who patiently proofreads my work
- ✓ My brother Mark T. Riley for editing and proofreading early versions of this book and offering suggestions
- ✓ To Thomas F. Ryan, editor and chief of the journal "The Undertoad" for offering me a regular outlet for my writing years ago. Without you Tom, this book would never have happened!
- ✓ My first employers when I entered the accounting profession many years ago, Peter Mandragouras, CPA and Jim Powers, CPA. They forever showed me that caring about the client is the very heart of our business

Contents

The New Tax Guide for Artists of Every Persuasion

Introduction

I must thank you for reading this book and tell you how I came to write it. This volume is a follow up to the esteemed *"New Tax Guide for Performers, Writers, Directors, Designers and Other Show Biz Folk"* written by R. Brendan Hanlon. I originally discovered Mr. Hanlon's book quite by accident while browsing in the Bleecker Street Bookstore many years ago during a trip to New York City. As an amateur guitar player and CPA I had a strong interest in all the arts and wondered why there seemed to be no books that addressed specifically the unique tax situations that folks in the arts encounter. I remember I was very excited when I saw the book and rushed to tell my wife that this was the book I had long been looking for. I purchased Mr. Hanlon's subsequent revisions, and as a testament to the book's value I would often have clients bring the book into their appointment with me. I periodically thought of contacting Mr. Hanlon but sadly never did. When I heard about Mr. Hanlon's death several years ago my first thought was that I hoped his valuable book did not pass away with him. I contacted Proscenium Publishers and offered to pick up authorship of the book. Although the book you hold is entirely rewritten I would like it to serve the same purpose of being an easy to read guide for the arts practitioner to help you understand your tax situation and thereby make the tax preparation process less onerous and most importantly SAVE TAX DOLLARS!

This book is not primarily intended to be a "how to prepare your income tax return" book (for this I recommend *J.K Lasser's™ Your Income Tax*). I feel strongly that the actual preparation of income tax returns for folks in the arts is best left to professionals because of the inherent complications. I think that good tax preparers and advisors should be able to save you more money than they charge by helping you with tax planning. Consequently, I am not necessarily going to attempt to give the reader line-by-line or form-by-form instructions–something guaranteed to put you to sleep! My goal is to give you an overall understanding of the unique aspects of taxation of people in the arts. By reading this book and using my deduction checklists I want you to do a better job at collecting the data through the year and be better prepared to present your tax information to your income tax advisor. I will use a lot of real life examples to illustrate the many situations an artist may encounter. By understanding your specific situation you will be better prepared to choose an appropriate income tax advisor. Keep in mind that no matter how good your tax advisor is, YOU are the one who has to develop a basic understanding of your taxable income and what is deductible, so that you are saving the proper receipts and documentation for your tax return.

I am going to focus mainly on your professional income and deductions and will only discuss in passing other income you may have, such as interest, dividends, capital gains, pensions, rents, and other deductions, such as mortgage interest, charitable contributions.

Our cast of characters throughout the book will be four artist friends whose professional lives will illustrate what the heck we are talking about:

1. Liz Brushstroke–Artist and College Professor. Liz is a tenured college professor but she also has an active life as an independent visual artist and is represented by a gallery in New York City and Dublin.

2. Ima Starr–Actor, model and writer. Ima (our only holdover from Mr. Hanlon's book) is very busy as both actor and model. She is also a part-time singer and has even written a book. She is a member of Actors' Equity Association and the Screen Actors Guild (SAG).

3. Sonny Phunky–Musician. Sonny is a freelance bass player and does some teaching on the side. He works both as an employee and as a contract player.

4. Guy Focal–Writer. Guy has a full-time magazine staff writer job but also has earnings writing freelance book reviews and articles for other publications, and he has published children's books.

Now the main thing that most folks worry about when they prepare their income taxes is the dreaded audit! Luckily, because of the Freedom of Information Act the Internal Revenue Service (IRS) is required to actually publish its internal audit guidelines. These Market Segment Specialization Program (MSSP) guides give us direct insight into what the IRS agent would be looking for in an audit. We will be discussing this in chapter 7.

Finally, I intend the book to be approached in the following fashion:

The book begins with two primary chapters everybody should read:

1. Income
2. What Can I Deduct?

Next choose the chapter that best describes your primary activity:

3. For Actors, Directors, Dancers and Other Show Biz Folks Only
4. For Musicians and Singers Only
5. For Visual Artists Only
6. For Writers Only

Finally, you will all read the last five chapters:

7. Setting up a Business Entity
8. The Audit Process, Recordkeeping and Your Taxpayer Rights
9. Choosing a Tax Advisor
10. Tax Planning
11. In Closing

The official Website for the book is www.arts-taxinfo.com. I will be posting links, updates to the book, tax law changes, tax tips and other information, so please bookmark the site!

1

Income

I will address the types of income a person involved in the arts might earn and introduce the most important point in the book: the differentiation between employment income and self-employment/contract income. In these days of multidisciplinary artists it is common for folks to have income and expenses from both employment and self-employment. According to this differentiation income and expenses will appear in different places on the income tax return. But first things first: *What is income?*

In essence, income is practically everything of value you receive in exchange for your products or services as a performer, visual artist or writer (hereafter referred to as "artist"). You can be "paid" in cash, services, or property—you can even have barter income. Taxable income may or may not be reported on a tax form such as a 1099 or W–2 at year-end. As well as the obvious form of cash payments for services directly performed or artwork delivered, your income may come in the form of "free" merchandise that a company gives you in exchange for a product endorsement. Actors often receive free or discounted products in exchange for the use of their name in advertisements. Musicians receive free merchandise for endorsing a particular instrument, brand of strings or other supplies. The types of activities and/or products that the artist may receive income from includes:

- ✓ Book publishing
- ✓ Recording
- ✓ Acting
- ✓ Product endorsements (including samples of the products endorsed)
- ✓ Personal appearances
- ✓ Sales of artwork
- ✓ Performance art
- ✓ Modeling
- ✓ Voice overs
- ✓ Touring
- ✓ Dance performances
- ✓ Choreography
- ✓ Lecturing

✓ Teaching
✓ Master classes
✓ Instructional videos
✓ Commissions
✓ Studio and art work rentals
✓ Stipends
✓ Website design fees
✓ Publication of articles
✓ Sales or rental of photographs
✓ Sales of CDs
✓ Sales of videos
✓ Directing
✓ Consulting
✓ Television and radio appearances

While not exhaustive the list gives a sense of the many activities that produce taxable income for the artist. These types of professional income will be added to your other income, whether *unearned income* such as interest, dividends, capital gains, rental income, alimony, prizes, unemployment income, or other *earned income* that is unrelated to your professional life, for instance, the musician that moonlights as a music store clerk or the actor who works as a waiter. These types of *unearned income* and unrelated *earned income* are handled on your income tax return in exactly the same fashion as they would be on anybody else's income tax return. It is with your professional income that things diverge.

What Type of Income Is It and Why? — Employee Wages vs. Contract Income

It is important to understand the difference between being paid as an employee who receives a form W–2 and receiving income for self-employment or as a contractor that is typically reported on a form 1099–MISC (this is sometimes referred to as "freelance" income). When you are paid as an employee on a W–2, the employer withholds federal, state and local (if applicable) income tax as well as the FICA taxes, Social Security and Medicare. If you are hired and paid as a contract worker, you will receive a form 1099–MISC at year-end and generally no taxes have been withheld. Understanding this distinction is critical because it determines how and where your income will be reported and where your professional expenses will be deducted. It is significant because if you have a substantial amount of contract income, you can end up the year with a large amount of income for which no taxes have been paid yet!

So what and who decides how your income is going to be treated? Generally the payer/employer will decide whether you are a contractor or employee. He or she will use the IRS rules cited below to arrive at the handling of your situation. In many cases the decision is fairly obvious. The key to whether someone is an employee or a contractor rests largely on how much independence the worker has or conversely how much control the person hiring the artist has over how the artist performs his or her duties. IRS publication 15–A discusses the three-part test that establishes the distinction between the employee and the independent contractor:

In any employee-independent contractor determination, all information that provides evidence of the degree of control and the degree of independence must be considered.

Facts that provide evidence of the degree of control and independence fall into three categories: behavioral control, financial control, and the type of relationship of the parties as shown below.

1. ***Behavioral control.*** *Facts that show whether the business has a right to direct and control how the worker does the task for which the worker is hired include the type and degree of-*

   Instructions the business gives the worker. An employee is generally subject to the business' instructions about when, where, and how to work. All of the following are examples of types of instructions about how to do work:

   - *When and where to do the work*
   - *What tools or equipment to use*
   - *What workers to hire or to assist with the work*
   - *Where to purchase supplies and services*
   - *What work must be performed by a specified individual*
   - *What order or sequence to follow*

   The amount of instruction needed varies among different jobs. Even if no instructions are given, sufficient behavioral control may exist if the employer has the right to control how the work results are achieved. A business may lack the knowledge to instruct some highly specialized professionals; in other cases, the task may require little or no instruction. The key consideration is whether the business has retained the right to control the details of a worker's performance or instead has given up that right.

   Training the business gives the worker. An employee may be trained to perform services in a particular manner. Independent contractors ordinarily use their own methods.

2. ***Financial control.*** *Facts that show whether the business has a right to control the business aspects of the worker's job include:*

    - *The extent to which the worker has unreimbursed business expenses. Independent contractors are more likely to have unreimbursed expenses than are employees. Fixed ongoing costs that are incurred regardless of whether work is currently being performed are especially important. However, employees may also incur unreimbursed expenses in connection with the services they perform for their business.*

    - *The extent of the worker's investment. An independent contractor often has a significant investment in the facilities he or she uses in performing services for someone else. However, a significant investment is not necessary for independent contractor status.*
    - *The extent to which the worker makes services available to the relevant market. An independent contractor is generally free to seek out business opportunities. Independent contractors often advertise, maintain a visible business location, and are available to work in the relevant market.*

    - *How the business pays the worker. An employee is generally guaranteed a regular wage amount for an hourly, weekly, or other period of time. This usually indicates that a worker is an employee, even when the wage or salary is supplemented by a commission. An independent contractor is usually paid by a flat fee for the job. However, it is common in some professions, such as law, to pay independent contractors hourly.*

    - *The extent to which the worker can realize a profit or loss. An independent contractor can make a profit or loss.*

3. ***Type of relationship.*** *Facts that show the parties' type of relationship include:*

    Written contracts describing the relationship the parties intended to create.

    Whether the business provides the worker with employee-type benefits, such as insurance, a pension plan, vacation pay, or sick pay.

    - *The permanency of the relationship. If you engage a worker with the expectation that the relationship will continue indefinitely, rather than for a specific project or period, this is generally considered evidence that your intent was to create an employer-employee relationship.*

> - *The extent to which services performed by the worker are a key aspect of the regular business of the company. If a worker provides services that are a key aspect of your regular business activity, it is more likely that you will have the right to direct and control his or her activities. For example, if a law firm hires an attorney, it is likely that it will present the attorney's work as its own and would have the right to control or direct that work. This would indicate an employer-employee relationship.*

So let's look at some examples of how these IRS rules might play out in your life.

Example One: Actor Ima Starr recently appeared in a production of *Godspell* at the Goodwrench Theatre in Philadelphia where she was obviously under the direct control of the production company and the theatre. She also did some modeling and a product endorsement for which she received contractor income. At year-end she will receive a W–2 for her work at the Goodwrench Theatre and for her modeling work may receive either a W–2 or a 1099–MISC form depending on how the agency treats the situation.

Example Two: Our good friend and musician Sonny Phunky signed to do a national tour playing with a famous rock band. He was considered to be an employee and received a W–2 from the band's production company at year-end. In the same year he gave private lessons, did some occasional studio work; played club dates and did other things that were considered contractor income. Sonny will not necessarily receive 1099s for all this income, for example his students would not issue him a 1099.

Example Three: Next is our painter, Liz Brushstroke. Liz is a tenured professor of art at a local college for whom she is an employee. Liz sells her independently produced artwork through a prominent New York City and Dublin art gallery. Sales of her artwork generate self-employment income for Liz as she is clearly not under the control of the gallery owner in any way. At year-end she will receive her W–2 from the college. She will probably not receive any tax form from the gallery, as her income was derived from the sale of tangible property.

Example Four: Finally we will visit our writer friend Guy Focal. In his regular job Guy is a staff writer for *Swamp Life Monthly*, a magazine in Louisiana that celebrates living life on the swamp. As a staff writer Guy reports daily to the magazine offices in New Orleans, he uses equipment owned by the magazine, the magazine reimburses Guy for his incidental expenses, and he is given assignments and deadlines for articles and features to write. This work is clearly an employment situation. In his spare time Guy writes and publishes children's books and does freelance book reviews and articles for other publications. Any royalties from his children's book sales will be self-employment income, as will income from his freelance writing (though it could be employment income). Both of these activities are clearly independently produced. At the end of the year Guy will receive a W–2 from Swamp Life Magazine Inc., a 1099–MISC from the publisher (or agent) of his children's books for his royalties income and 1099–MISC forms from the various magazines that published his reviews and articles.

Why are we spending so much time on this esoteric IRS stuff, and how does this relate to your activities as an artist? One can grasp that the artist will often have in a single year both employment (W–2) AND contractor/freelance (1099–MISC) income. As we will soon see, the type of income you receive will guide how and where the income is reported on your income tax return and, most importantly, how and where the expenses are deducted.

The Mysteries of the W–2 Revealed

W–2s are sometimes issued on the completion of a particular job, but are supposed to be received no later than January 31 of the following year. Keep in mind that it is up to you to let your various employers know your correct address. I recommend that artists keep a diary of their employers during the year as the number of W–2s due can add up and it is easy to forget one. Start a checklist at the beginning of the year (why not use the one found in the appendix of this very volume or download the one from the website www.arts-taxinfo.com) so you can use it as a guide at year-end. As you do this, be sure to retain copies of all pay stubs. Note not only of the employer but also the name of the payroll company, since the W–2 may be issued in the payroll company's name. You may also receive unexpected W–2s for residual work in prior years (an issue for actors and musicians). I advise clients who move often to obtain a central, stable mailing address for W–2s and other tax forms, such as a manager's, business agent's or accountant's address. Some artists use a family address or a post office or private mailbox that can be instructed to forward mail to their current address.

The following is a key to the 21 boxes found on the 2001 W–2 form:

> Box 1   Federal taxable wages and tips-This is where federal taxable wages are reported; other taxable fringe benefits may be reported here.
>
> Box 2   Federal income tax withheld-On this line is the amount of federal income taxes withheld on your income.

Boxes 3, 4 & 7   Social Security wages and withholdings-Social Security taxes are withheld at a rate of 6.2%, capped on the first $80,400 in 2001 (adjusted annually).

Boxes 5 & 6   Medicare wages and tax withholdings-Medicare taxes are withheld at a rate of 1.45% with no cap.

Box 8   Allocated tips-If you worked in a restaurant with at least 10 employees your employer will report your share of 8% of gross receipts unless you reported tips at least equal to that share.

Box 9   Advance earned income payments-If you filed form W-5 asking for part of the credit to be added to your wages it will be included here.

Box 10   Dependent care benefits-Advances from your employer for dependent care benefits under a qualifying plan.

Box 11   Nonqualified plan distributions-Distributions for nonqualified deferred compensation plans.

Box 12 (A-D)   Catch-all box for such things as retirement plans, life insurance, moving expenses, travel allowance reimbursements, etc. Coding printed on back of your W–2 indicates exactly what the items in this box pertain to.

Box 13   Checkboxes to inform the IRS of pension plan availability and other information

Box 14   Miscellaneous payments-Where employers can choose to put other items they wish to report to the employee.

Boxes 15-20   State and local tax information-These boxes will show your state and local taxable income as well as state and local taxes withheld (if applicable).

The taxable income amounts totaled from all your W–2s in the year will be reported on line 7 of your 1040.

So now let's look at the W–2 live and in person:

Our resident actor Ima Starr receives a W–2 from her work at the well-known Goodwrench Dinner Theatre in Philadelphia. Even though Ima resides in New York City, the fact that she is performing in Philadelphia means she is subject not only to Pennsylvania state tax but also to a Philadelphia municipal tax. This may mean that Ima will have to file Pennsylvania AND Philadelphia income tax returns at year-end (see W–2 boxes 16-21). Note that in box 15 the "Pension Plan" box is checked, which indicates to the IRS that Ima has a retirement plan available to her; in this case it is her Actors Equity Association union plan. This fact will limit her ability to take an IRA deduction.

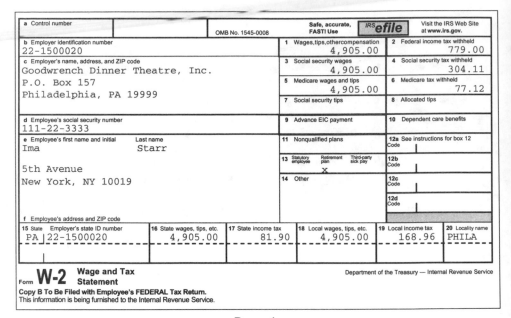

a Control number			Safe, accurate, FAST! Use	IRS *efile*	Visit the IRS Web Site at www.irs.gov.

OMB No. 1545-0008

b Employer identification number	1 Wages, tips, other compensation	2 Federal income tax withheld
22-1500020	4,905.00	779.00

c Employer's name, address, and ZIP code	3 Social security wages	4 Social security tax withheld
Goodwrench Dinner Theatre, Inc.	4,905.00	304.11
P.O. Box 157	5 Medicare wages and tips	6 Medicare tax withheld
Philadelphia, PA 19999	4,905.00	77.12
	7 Social security tips	8 Allocated tips

d Employee's social security number	9 Advance EIC payment	10 Dependent care benefits
111-22-3333		

e Employee's first name and initial Last name	11 Nonqualified plans	12a See instructions for box 12 Code
Ima Starr		
	13 Statutory employee Retirement plan Third-party sick pay X	12b Code
5th Avenue	14 Other	12c Code
New York, NY 10019		12d Code

f Employee's address and ZIP code

15 State Employer's state ID number	16 State wages, tips, etc.	17 State income tax	18 Local wages, tips, etc.	19 Local income tax	20 Locality name
PA 22-1500020	4,905.00	81.90	4,905.00	168.96	PHILA

Form **W-2** Wage and Tax Statement   Department of the Treasury — Internal Revenue Service

Copy B To Be Filed with Employee's FEDERAL Tax Return.
This information is being furnished to the Internal Revenue Service.

PLATE 1

Our bass player musician Sonny Phunky has been hired to play on a national tour with the Butterball Kings rock band. In this case Sonny was considered an employee and the Butterball Kings, Inc., production company was his employer. Prior to their tour, the group rehearsed in New York City for three weeks. Sonny is not a New York City resident so he was given a $300 per diem amount by the production company to cover his living expenses. This is indicated in box 12A with a code "L." Sonny rehearsed with the Butterball Kings for 3 weeks in New York City. The IRS per diem in Manhattan for 2001 was $244 per day (lodging of $198 and meals of $46). Therefore Sonny's per diem was higher than the IRS approved rate by $56 a day. In box 12A you will see the amount of $5,124 ($6,300 less $1,176). The $5,124 is the actual IRS approved per diem rate for 3 weeks in Manhattan ($244 × 21 days). The excess $1,176 will be reported as taxable wages in Box 1 on Sonny's W–2. In other words Sonny has to pay taxes on the per diem rate paid to him that is higher than what the IRS allows. If he has the receipts to back up the additional deduction, he can certainly write off living expenses to offset the extra $1,176 in income. You will also note that Sonny, even thought he is a resident of Rockridge, Maine, will be paying New York state taxes on this income and may need to file a New York income tax return.

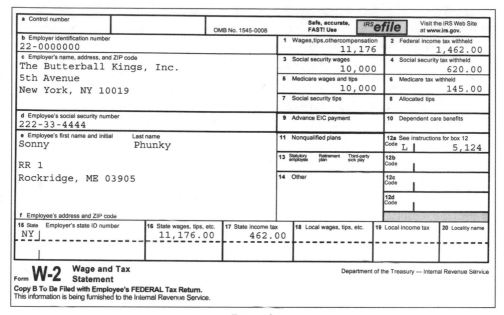

PLATE 2

While we are reviewing what the W–2 tells us (and the IRS), it is interesting to note what the W–2 does *not* tell us. It does not indicate when the money was earned, how long the artist worked, the weekly gross, often because the issuer will be a generic payroll service or production company it does not indicate who the artist was working for. Although the Social Security ceiling is $80,400 (adjusted annually) of income in 2001, if the artist works for a number of different employers and earns more than that amount he or she will quite likely overpay into Social Security. This amount of overpayment will be refunded when you file your 1040 at year-end.

As an employee you control the amount of federal income taxes withheld by filling out the federal form W-4 with the employer. This is something that your tax advisor can help you with. By calculating the total amount of expected annual income you can arrive at a reasonable estimation of what your withholdings should be.

In Search of Form 1099

While there are a multitude of different 1099 forms, including the common ones issued for interest and dividend income, the artist is mainly concerned with the 1099–MISC. The 1099–MISC is fairly straightforward with 13 self-explanatory boxes. The IRS requires payers issue the form 1099–MISC for each person to whom they pay at least $10 in gross royalty payments or $600 for services in the course of a calendar year. If you receive a form 1099–MISC for your services as an artist you are generally considered self-employed, especially if these services constitute a substantial part of your income for the year. You may even be issuing a form 1099–MISC *yourself,* if you have paid anyone in excess of $600 for personal services or compensation. Let's look at a few examples of 1099 forms that the artist might receive. Our author Guy Focal may receive a 1099 from his children's book publisher that looks like this:

			CORRECTED (if checked)		
PAYER'S name, street address, city, state, and ZIP code		1 Rents	OMB No. 1545-0115		
		$			Miscellaneous Income
Kids are Great Publishers, Inc. Main Street New York NY 10019		2 Royalties	**2001**		
		$ 3,254.00	Form **1099-MISC**		
		3 Other income	4 Federal income tax withheld		Copy B For Recipient
		$	$		
PAYER'S Federal identification number	RECIPIENT'S identification number	5 Fishing boat proceeds	6 Medical and health care payments		
04-0000000	333-44-5555	$	$		This is important tax information and is being furnished to the Internal Revenue Service. If you are required to file a return, a negligence penalty or other sanction may be imposed on you if this income is taxable and the IRS determines that it has not been reported.
RECIPIENT'S name		7 Nonemployee compensation	8 Substitute payments in lieu of dividends or interest		
Guy Focal		$	$		
Street address (including apt. no.)		9 Payer made direct sales of $5,000 or more of consumer products to a buyer (recipient) for resale	10 Crop insurance proceeds		
Basin Street			$		
City, state, and ZIP code New Orleans, LA 23000		11	12		
Account number (optional)		13 Excess golden parachute payments	14 Gross proceeds paid to an attorney		
		$	$		
15		16 State tax withheld	17 State/Payer's state no.	18 State income	
		$		$	
		$		$	
Form **1099-MISC**		(Keep for your records.)		Department of the Treasury - Internal Revenue Service	

PLATE 3

Guy will report this income on the federal form Schedule C, not on the often and incorrectly used Schedule E (there is a line on federal Schedule E for royalties, and it is not uncommon to see royalties for writers reported on that line but the royalties reported on the schedule E are gas, oil and mining royalties.) Royalty income for authors is considered self-employment income for tax purposes.

For some miscellaneous studio work that looked like this our friend and bass player Sonny got a 1099–MISC:

CORRECTED (if checked)			
PAYER'S name, street address, city, state, and ZIP code	**1** Rents	OMB No. 1545-0115	
Hogs Breath Recording Studio, LLC Main St Chicago, IL 22331	$ **2** Royalties $	**2001** Form **1099-MISC**	**Miscellaneous Income**
	3 Other income $	**4** Federal income tax withheld $	Copy B For Recipient
PAYER'S Federal identification number RECIPIENT'S identification number 30-4552222 222-33-4444	**5** Fishing boat proceeds $	**6** Medical and health care payments $	
RECIPIENT'S name Sonny Phunky	**7** Nonemployee compensation $ 2,150	**8** Substitute payments in lieu of dividends or interest $	This is important tax information and is being furnished to the Internal Revenue Service. If you are required to file a return, a negligence penalty or other sanction may be imposed on you if this income is taxable and the IRS determines that it has not been reported.
Street address (including apt. no.) RR 1	**9** Payer made direct sales of $5,000 or more of consumer products to a buyer (recipient) for resale	**10** Crop insurance proceeds $	
City, state, and ZIP code Rockridge, ME 03905	**11**	**12**	
Account number (optional)	**13** Excess golden parachute payments $	**14** Gross proceeds paid to an attorney $	
15	**16** State tax withheld $ $	**17** State/Payer's state no.	**18** State income $ $
Form **1099-MISC**	(Keep for your records.)		Department of the Treasury - Internal Revenue Service

PLATE 4

Sonny's studio work will be shown in box 7 as non-employee compensation and will be reported on Schedule C.

Ima Starr won a prize when she entered a contest while in Philadelphia. She won a historic, fully restored Yugo automobile that was worth $1,000. Her 1099–MISC will reflect this in box 3 and look like this:

CORRECTED (If checked)				
PAYER'S name, street address, city, state, and ZIP code	1 Rents $	OMB No. 1545-0115		
Muddy Mudskippers BBQ, Inc. Main St Philadelphia, PA 19999	2 Royalties $	**2001** Form **1099-MISC**	**Miscellaneous Income**	
	3 Other income $ 1,000	4 Federal income tax withheld $		**Copy B For Recipient**
PAYER'S Federal identification number RECIPIENT'S identification number	5 Fishing boat proceeds	6 Medical and health care payments		This is important tax information and is being furnished to the Internal Revenue Service. If you are required to file a return, a negligence penalty or other sanction may be imposed on you if this income is taxable and the IRS determines that it has not been reported.
22-3232320 111-22-3333	$	$		
RECIPIENT'S name	7 Nonemployee compensation	8 Substitute payments in lieu of dividends or interest		
Ima Starr	$	$		
Street address (including apt. no.)	9 Payer made direct sales of $5,000 or more of consumer products to a buyer (recipient) for resale	10 Crop insurance proceeds		
5th Avenue		$		
City, state, and ZIP code New York, NY 10019	11	12		
Account number (optional)	13 Excess golden parachute payments $	14 Gross proceeds paid to an attorney $		
15	16 State tax withheld $ $	17 State/Payer's state no.	18 State income $ $	
Form **1099-MISC**	(Keep for your records.)	Department of the Treasury - Internal Revenue Service		

PLATE 5

I cite this example because box 3 "Other" is often used as a real "catch all" box when the issuer does not know where to put a particular item. It is not uncommon to find products given in product endorsement situations put in here. In the case of Ms. Starr's Yugo, since she did not give any services in exchange, the value of the car is not considered self-employment income. If she had done a product endorsement, for example if she had done a commercial for Yugo, the value of the auto would be reported as self-employment income, because the product is being given in exchange for services, namely the endorsement.

Another point to bear in mind is that as an artist the IRS treats you as a "cash basis taxpayer." Cash basis means that generally speaking your income is the value of what you *receive* during the calendar year. So income reported on the 1099 form is not necessarily income for the recipient in the same year. For example, our musician Sonny did some studio work at the end of the year. The studio wanted the deduction on that year's tax return so they issued and mailed the check on December 31 and correctly put the payment on the 1099–MISC they issued to Sonny for that year (after all they had in fact paid it that year). Sonny did not receive the check until January 4 of the following year; consequently he does not have to consider that payment as income in the same year as the 1099 would indicate. In these cases the artist can show the income not received as an adjustment to the 1099 and add the income to his or her return in the subsequent year.

The Joys of Being Self-employed

So what does it mean to be self-employed and have self-employment income? Understand that when you receive a substantial part of your income reported on Form 1099 then you are considered self-employed. It is critical to understand how self-employment income is taxed. Self-employment income is subject to *two separate taxes* on your federal tax return: income tax and self-employment tax. Self-employment income is reported on federal Schedule C and self-employment tax is calculated on federal Form SE (for self-employment). The following diagram indicates how self-employment income is taxed on the 1040:

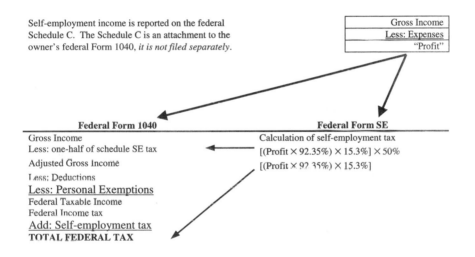

We can see from this diagram that income from self-employment is subject to two levels of taxation:

✓ The first is the 15.3% self-employment tax. This tax has 2 elements: 2.9% is Medicare tax and 12.4% is Social Security taxes that the IRS collects on behalf of the Social Security Administration. Medicare tax is calculated on all the self-employment income. Social Security tax is applied only on the first $80,400 of income in 2001 (adjusted annually). Remember that your personal exemptions and deductions for your home mortgage interest, real estate tax, and state taxes, etc., do not affect the calculation of this tax.

✓ The second level is the federal income tax.

Estimated Taxes

Because self-employment income will not generally be subject to withholding tax it is **very easy** to get into trouble and end up owing unexpected amounts of money on April 15. Therefore as a self-employed artist you will probably be required to pay estimated taxes quarterly. If a substantial amount of your income is going to be in the form of self-employment income, I say, get thee to a good tax advisor! Your tax advisor will help you estimate what your potential federal and state tax liability might be for the year. Keep in mind that your taxable income is your gross income LESS your expenses and deductions. Estimated taxes are paid quarterly on April 15, June 15, September 15 of the current year and January 15 of the following year on federal form 1040-ES. To make a reasonable estimate of your potential tax liability you have to be able to determine what your income related expenses are going to be. This is where the record keeping becomes vital (more on that later)!

So What's All the Hubbub, Bub!

The hubbub is that you must understand the mix of your W–2 and 1099 income to properly organize and be prepared to do your income taxes. Very few folks in the arts are involved purely in one activity; it's that multi-discipline *thang!*

Our own Ima Starr is a member of Actors' Equity Association and received multiple W–2 forms this year. These W–2s will be added up and put on line 7 of her 1040 income tax form. Her expenses associated with these activities will be found on Form 2106 – Employee Business Expense (more on that later). Ima is also the sultry lounge singer in the group The Blue Jazzbos. She published a tell-all book about her life in show business last year. That means she has three streams of self-employment income, one for music, one for writing and one for modeling! She must, to the best of her abilities, allocate her business expenses among these various activities, as they will need to be entered on various forms on her personal income tax return. She might even have to pay estimated income taxes on her self-employment income, especially if the movie rights for her book are sold!

In the world of the arts, actors play in rock bands, musicians write books, dancers perform and teach dance, visual artists teach and design websites, writers lecture and teach, etc. These various activities require you to compartmentalize your income and expenses to a certain degree. Next we will look at the other side of our equation: expenses and deductions.

2

What Can I Deduct?

In this chapter I will take a bird's eye view of expenses and deductions as they pertain to the artist to show how the IRS interprets the general deductibility of the more common expenses that all artists have, such as automobile use, travel, meals, entertainment, and the controversial home office. I will also look at the Qualified Performing Artists (QPA) provision, start up costs, as well as the also controversial "hobby loss" rules. Following chapters will deal more specifically with the deductible expenses in the various disciplines, but for now let's get an overview.

The heart of saving money on your tax return is making sure you do not miss any deductions or expenses. As we have said, the artist has to be concerned about the type of income the deduction is associated with. This is the core of where the deduction goes on the tax return; i.e., does this expense relate to W–2 employment earnings or 1099 self-employment income?

Let's look at what the IRS says regarding expense deductions in general in its Publication 583:

> You can deduct business expenses on your income tax return. These are the current operating costs of running your business. To be deductible, a business expense must be both ordinary and necessary. An ordinary expense is one that is common and accepted in your field of business, trade, or profession. A necessary expense is one that is helpful and appropriate for your business, trade, or profession. An expense does not have to be indispensable to be considered necessary.

And from Publication 334:

> You cannot deduct expenses that are lavish or extravagant under the circumstances.

So we can see the IRS has only three fairly simple criteria for deductible business expenses:

1. Must be incurred in connection with your trade, business, or profession.
2. Must be ordinary and necessary.
3. Must not be lavish or extravagant.

As I mentioned in the last chapter, as an artist you are treated as what the IRS calls a "cash basis taxpayer," which means generally speaking your expenses and deductions are anything you expend money or value on during the calendar year. If you pay for a tax-deductible expense via check, cash, barter, or charge card (even if you don't pay off the credit card until the following year) the expense will qualify as a deduction in the current year. This all seems straightforward but as the saying goes, "The devil is in the details."

First, let's tackle the matter of whether the deduction is related to employment (W–2) income or self-employment (Form 1099) income. While the types of expenses that are deductible will usually not change between employment and self-employment, the manner in which the deduction is taken and its effect on your tax return can be critical. Important point: the deductibility of specific items can be largely identical for employees and for the self-employed; it is basically a mechanical matter as to how they are treated during the preparation of the income tax return. Put another way, the "employee" artist might and will indeed often have the exact group of deductions as the "self-employed" artist. The following chart illustrates the flow of income and deductions:

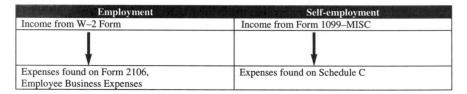

Employment	Self-employment
Income from W–2 Form	Income from Form 1099–MISC
Expenses found on Form 2106, Employee Business Expenses	Expenses found on Schedule C

So what is the key difference between these two methods? Form 2106 will usually become an itemized deduction on Schedule A (except for the Qualified Performing Artist) of the 1040 and be subject to a 2% floor. In other words, if your adjusted gross income is $100,000 you will *automatically* lose $2,000 ($100,000 × 2%) of your professional expenses. In addition, if the artist does not have any other itemized deductions, such as home mortgage interest, real estate taxes, state tax payments, then the value of the employee business expenses can be reduced even further. On the other hand deductions against self-employment income are written off dollar for dollar directly against the self-employment income on the Schedule C.

Let's see how this plays out with our four artists:

Ima Starr is a member of Actors' Equity so the bulk of her annual income is reported on the W–2 forms she received. That means that all of her acting expenses will be reported on Form 2106 as employee business expenses. For self-employment Ima sings in a jazz group, did some modeling and even wrote a book! She and her accountant will be allocating expenses associated with these activities to her Schedule C. These expenses might include auto usage, publications, music equipment purchase, CDs, home office. It is not always easy to figure out this "allocation" I refer to. What if all of Ima Starr's income were earned only in New York City where she lives? By which I mean all the acting jobs, music gigs, modeling assignments, etc., are in NYC. How does one allocate expenses in a situation like that? The answer is-very carefully and systematically! In cases where a clear-cut differentiation is impossible, try for a methodical and consistent approach. This might be done, by allocating the expenses according to income received, days worked, or some other formula. In other words, first assign the expenses you can clearly and directly associate with each type of income, then allocate general expenses via a formula. It is clear; Ima's Actors' Equity dues would be an expense on Form 2106 against her employment income. The sound system and CDs she purchased for her singing career would be deducted against her self-employment income. For her home office and her new Powerbook® computer it can be argued that they benefit all her activities equally, so these expenses might be allocated according to an income-based formula (the formula the IRS prefers). If 25% of her gross earnings were from her self-employment activities, she may choose to assign 25% of her home office and computer expenses to her Schedule C. While this gross income method is not perfect, it is logical, defensible and easy to explain in an IRS audit situation!

Now, our bass player Sonny Phunky. Let's deal with just four of Sonny's expense line items for the year: the purchase of a new bass guitar, music supplies, auto mileage, travel & meals.

When Sonny arrives at his accountant's office he will have his W–2 from Butterball Kings, Inc., for his tour. He will also have 1099–MISC forms for some of his studio work and gigs. And he will have some unreported income from teaching the bass guitar to his students. So how will Sonny and his accountant differentiate the expenses for these items on the tax return? It turns out that the Butterball Kings specifically requested that he play a chartreuse colored bass to match their other stage equipment, which forced Sonny to purchase a new custom painted bass guitar for the tour. This would be grounds for Sonny's accountant to write off (*depreciate*–more on this later) the new bass against his W–2 by using Form 2106. In regard to the music supplies, Sonny and his accountant may choose to take all the expenses purchased during his time with the Butterball Kings as a deduction against the W–2, since that was his primary professional activity in that time frame. They would probably use the same approach for auto mileage. Sonny's use of his car to drive from Maine to NYC, for transportation in and around New York while he was in the city for rehearsals could all be used as a deduction against the W–2.

For his living expenses while in NYC, Sonny may not have any deductions. You will remember that the Butterball Kings' W–2 indicated to the IRS (Box 13-Code L) that Sonny was given a per diem allowance to cover them. If this allowance did cover all his meals and lodging, then Sonny would have no write-off for these expenses. If this allowance was less than he actually paid to be in NYC then he might have an additional write-off of the amount over and above the allowance.

Sonny's expenses for the rest of the year for music supplies, travel, mileage to the studio and gigs, etc., would become a deduction on his Schedule C against his self-employment income. We can see from this example that Sonny will have many of the same expense line items on both his 2106 and his Schedule C forms.

Let's look at our visual artist Liz. As a college professor she may have no deductions at all because the college would probably be supplying all her teaching materials. But Liz would indeed have expenses for her work as an independent artist. Her expenses for framing, art supplies, her home studio, mileage to visit the gallery in NYC and travel to the gallery in Dublin would all be deductions on her Schedule C form.

Finally, our writer, Guy. The magazine Guy works for would probably be supplying all his materials and equipment so he may have no deductions at all against his W–2. The magazine will also generally be reimbursing Guy for his auto use on the job. Guy would indeed have expenses for his work as an independent writer. Which might include the use of a home office, purchase of books, travel, and home computer. These expenses would appear on Schedule C as deduction against his royalties and other freelance writing income.

It's time to delve into some of the larger expense line items that typically affect all artists.

The Automobile

The use of your car for business is often the most common expense the artist has and often the single largest deduction. The IRS has two basic methods for writing off the business use of your automobile. It allows you to use either the annually adjusted IRS standard mileage rate or the actual expenses of operating your car. In Publication 334 the IRS sums it up in the following language:

> *For local transportation or overnight travel by car or truck, you generally can use one of the following methods to figure your expenses.*

1. Standard mileage rate.

Standard mileage rate. You may be able to use the standard mileage rate to figure the deductible costs of operating your car, van, pickup, or panel truck for business purposes. For 2001, the standard mileage rate is 34 1/2 cents (this is adjusted annually) a mile for all business miles.

Caution. If you choose to use the standard mileage rate for a year, you cannot deduct your actual expenses for that year except for business-related parking fees and tolls.

Choosing the standard mileage rate. If you want to use the standard mileage rate for a car or truck you own, you must choose to use it in the first year the car is available for use in your business. In later years, you can choose to use either the standard mileage rate or actual expenses.

If you want to use the standard mileage rate for a car you lease, you must choose to use it for the entire lease period. For leases that began on or before December 31, 1997, the standard mileage rate must be used for the entire portion of the lease period (including renewals) after that date.

Standard mileage rate not allowed. You cannot use the standard mileage rate if you:

1. *Use the car for hire (such as a taxi),*
2. *Operate two or more cars at the same time,*
3. *Claimed a depreciation deduction using ACRS or MACRS in an earlier year,*
4. *Claimed a section 179 deduction on the car,*
5. *Claimed actual car expenses after 1997 for a car you leased, or*
6. *Are a rural mail carrier who received a qualified reimbursement.*

Parking fees and tolls. In addition to using the standard mileage rate, you can deduct any business-related parking fees and tolls. (Parking fees you pay to park your car at your place of work are nondeductible commuting expenses.)

2. Actual Expenses

Actual expenses. If you do not choose to use the standard mileage rate, you may be able to deduct your actual car or truck expenses. TIP. If you qualify to use both methods, figure your deduction both ways to see which gives you a larger deduction.

Actual car expenses include the costs of the following items:

Depreciation	*Lease Payments*	*Registration Fees*
Garage Rent	*Licenses*	*Repairs*
Gas	*Oil*	*Tires*
Insurance	*Parking Fees*	*Tolls*

If you use your vehicle for both business and personal purposes, you must divide your expenses between business and personal use. You can divide based on the miles driven for each purpose.

Example: *You are the musician. You drove your van 20,000 miles during the year. 16,000 miles were for going to gigs including delivering equipment and 4,000 miles were for personal use. You can claim only 80% (16,000/20,000) of the cost of operating your van as a business expense.*

The easiest method for most folks is to use the generous IRS standard mileage allowance. This option does not require retention of receipts of any kind. All you need to have is a record in your diary or appointment book of business miles driven.

As a rule, personal miles (going to the grocery store, the dentist, out to dinner, etc.) and commuting mileage are generally not deductible. If you have a legitimate office at home it tends to make all business miles deductible, after all there can be no commute if you work at home. Otherwise your commute would normally be the first and last trip every day. To illustrate, if our visual artist Liz left her college job at noon, drove to pick up some art supplies, stopped by to speak to a gallery owner, then drove back to school to check in before going home, all her miles from the time she left school until she arrived back at school would be deductible business miles; the balance would be non-deductible commuting miles.

By keeping an accurate appointment book you should have all the info you need to estimate your business miles.

The Home Office

The home office has been a contentious subject among tax professionals for a number of years, but with recent legislation, it has clearly returned to its rightful place as an allowable deduction for many folks in all aspects of the arts. If you use a room (or rooms) in your home exclusively as your office AND you have no other office space available to you, you will most likely qualify for the home office deduction. To qualify as a deductible home office the space must generally be:

1. The principal place of business,
2. The place where the taxpayer meets with clients, customers or colleagues

The room can be used as an office, a storage area for equipment, manuscripts and supplies, for recordkeeping for the business, marketing, etc. For the actor, dancer, filmmaker, and musician it can be a space for keeping business records, preparing correspondence, promotional activities, rehearsing and library/manuscript storage. For the writer and visual artist the home office is where you write and paint or sculpt. It can be a home darkroom for the photographer.

The home office is a fairly straightforward deduction to calculate on federal Form 8829. It simply utilizes a formula based on the square footage of the business portion (the home office) of your home vs. the total square footage of the house or apartment and then applies that percentage to all associated costs. The costs might be rent, mortgage interest, real estate taxes, condo fees, utilities, insurance, repairs, etc. If you own your own home, you can even depreciate that portion of your house for an additional write-off.

For example:

	Business use (square footage)	250
	Total square footage of home	1250
	Business use percentage (250/1250)	20%
Mortgage Interest	$7,500	
Real Estate Tax	$2,500	
Utilities	$1,820	
Water & Sewer	$820	
Insurance	$400	
Repairs	$225	
Total home expenses	$13,265	
	Potential home office deduction: ($13,265 × 20%)	**$2,653**

Other rules that come into play here include the "exclusive use" requirement. This rule states that the home office must be used only for the business – no "mixed use" is allowed. Put another way the home office or studio cannot be a part of a larger room, such as the living room, unless the business part is partitioned off somehow. Be careful when allocating home office expense. The Internal Revenue Service could decide that one of the activities is really a "hobby" and not a legitimate business and then the entire home office will be blown off the return. Why? Because it would no longer be exclusive use.

For instance if Ima Starr's accountant felt that her book writing would not pass muster as a true business, he would do well to not allocate any home office expense to it.

A note of warning when you own your own home and you start utilizing the home office deduction, you are essentially converting a portion of your home into a business property. By doing this you may be putting the $250,000/$500,000 exclusion on the sale of a principal residence in jeopardy. Depending on your situation this can be a strong argument against using the home office deduction. Be sure to discuss this with your qualified tax advisor, especially if you are planning on selling your home in the near future.

Equipment Purchases and Depreciation & Amortization of Recordings, Films & Books

This first section concerns the purchase of equipment used by the artist. It pertains to the purchase of any large assets such as computers, printers, handheld computers, personal digital assistants (PDAs), musical instruments and equipment, cameras and photographic equipment, sculptor's welding equipment, presses or other devices used by visual artists, video cameras and equipment, sound and audio devices. The purchase of the violin or computer is considered intrinsically unlike paying the phone bill in that when you purchase the violin or computer it will have a life beyond the year bought, unlike the phone service, which has no "life." Therefore depreciation of equipment is a method of dividing the cost of the asset over its IRS defined "useful life" and deducting it a little bit at a time, year by year, until the entire purchase price has been deducted.

In Publication 334 the IRS discusses depreciation this way:

> *If property you acquire to use in your business is expected to last more than one year, you generally cannot deduct the entire cost as a business expense in the year you acquire it. You must spread the cost over more than one tax year and deduct part of it each year on Schedule C, C-EZ or Form 2106. This method of deducting the cost of business property is called depreciation.*
>
> **What can be depreciated?** *You can depreciate property if it meets all the following requirements.*
>
> ✓ *It must be used in business or held to produce income.*
> ✓ *It must be expected to last more than one year. In other words, it must have a useful life that extends substantially beyond the year it is placed in service.*
> ✓ *It must be something that wears out, decays, gets used up, becomes obsolete, or loses its value from natural causes.*

What cannot be depreciated? You cannot depreciate any of the following items.

✓ *Property placed in service and disposed of in the same year.*
✓ *Inventory.*
✓ *Land.*
✓ *Repairs and replacements that do not increase the value of your property, make it more useful, or lengthen its useful life. You can deduct these amounts on Schedule C, C-EZ or Form 2106.*

Depreciation method. *The method for depreciating most tangible property placed in service after 1986 is called the Modified Accelerated Cost Recovery System (MACRS). (Tangible property is property you can see or touch.) MACRS is discussed in detail in Publication 946.*

Section 179 deduction. *You can choose to deduct a limited amount (for 2001, up to $24,000) of the cost of certain depreciable property in the year you buy it for use in your business. This deduction is known as the "section 179 deduction." For more information, see Publication 946. It explains what costs you can and cannot deduct, how to figure the deduction, and when to recapture the deduction.*

Listed property. *Listed property is any of the following.*

✓ *Most passenger automobiles.*
✓ *Most other property used for transportation.*
✓ *Any property of a type generally used for entertainment, recreation, or amusement.*
✓ *Certain computer and related peripheral equipment.*
✓ *Any cellular telephone (or similar telecommunications equipment).*

You must follow additional rules and recordkeeping requirements when depreciating listed property. For more information about listed property, see Publication 946.

What are the typical "lives" of commonly purchased assets according to the IRS?

✓ Computer and technology type assets = 5 years
✓ Automobiles and light trucks = 5 years
✓ Office furniture, fixtures, musical instruments and machinery = 7 years
✓ Commercial real estate = 39 years

Depreciation is calculated and reported on Form 4562, and is then carried either to the Schedule C if written off against self-employment income, or the Form 2106 if deducted against W–2 employment earnings.

A common depreciation/deduction question that comes up in the arts concerns the purchase of collectables and other antiques. For the actor or director it can be the acquisition of a film or theatre prop or poster, for the musician it can be an antique instrument, for the visual artist it could be a piece of artwork and for the writer it may be a first edition book. While these items may be related directly to your profession the IRS generally feels such items are personal in nature and not deductible or subject to depreciation. That is because they are often not used directly in the artist's profession, but are decorative in nature. The other reason the IRS does not allow a deduction is because the nature of a collectable is to appreciate in value, not depreciate. The IRS has lost several court cases over a musician writing-off of an antique instrument. In two cases it was critical that the musician used the instrument in actual performance and recording. By doing this one taxpayer argued that the use of the bass viol did diminish the value of the instrument due to the perspiration from the performer's hands and through oxidation of the wood. In tax court cases the IRS can either agree with the court or not agree. In these cases, the IRS did not acquiesce in the decisions of the tax court. So you cannot rely on these court rulings as a precedent. If you do decide to depreciate an antique or collectable be sure that you are actually using it in your job as an artist and prepare for an argument!

The creation of film, videos, books and recordings follows similar concepts as depreciation: they are assumed to have some value beyond the year in which they are created and are written off over a period of time. In the case of film and recordings, the term used is *amortization*. The total cost of creating the film or recording is capitalized and then written off using one of two IRS approved formulas. Unlike the purchase of a computer, the IRS does not define a pre-determined life for film and recordings. The two methods are:

1. The income forecast method–the creator estimates the amount and timing of the income stream from sales of the film, book or recording and expenses the costs associated with the creation or acquisition over that period of time. For instance, if the recording or film cost $50,000 to produce and the income was expected to be earned over 3 years in the following formula 65%–25%–10% then the $50,000 would be written off $32,500–$12,500–$5,000.
2. Straight-line over the useful life—if the creator expects the film, book or recording will have a useful life of 4 years then he or she would divide the $50,000 production cost by 4 and take approximately $12,500 in expense each year.

An exception to the above rule concerns music videos. If the artist creates a music video to be used primarily for shopping the artist to record companies, then the cost of the video is immediately deductible as advertising expense, not subject to amortization.

Travel and Meal Expenses

After the business use of the automobile, travel can be the next most common and thorny issue for the artist. Before we discuss travel for the artist let's see what the IRS says about business travel in its Publication 463 which includes an excellent chart (Table 1) of what types of items are deductible:

> *Deductible travel expenses include those ordinary and necessary expenses you have when you travel away from home on business. The type of expense you can deduct depends on the facts and your circumstances.*
>
> *Table 1 summarizes travel expenses you may be able to deduct. You may have other deductible travel expenses that are not covered there, depending on the facts and your circumstances.*
>
> **Records.** *When you travel away from home on business, you should keep records of all the expenses you have and any advances you receive from your employer. You can use a log, diary, notebook, or any other written record to keep track of your expenses.*
>
> **Travel expenses for another individual.** *If a spouse, dependent, or other individual goes with you (or your employee) on a business trip or to a business convention, you generally cannot deduct his or her travel expenses.*
>
> **Employee.** *You can deduct the travel expenses you have for an accompanying individual if that individual:*
>
> ✓ *Is your employee,*
> ✓ *Has a bona fide business purpose for the travel, and*
> ✓ *Would otherwise be allowed to deduct the travel expenses.*
>
> **Business associate.** *If a business associate travels with you and meets the conditions in (2) and (3) above, you can claim the deductible travel expenses you have for that person. A business associate is someone with whom you could reasonably expect to actively conduct business. A business associate can be a current or prospective (likely to become) customer, client, supplier, employee, agent, partner, or professional advisor.*
>
> **Bona fide business purpose.** *For a bona fide business purpose to exist, you must prove a real business purpose for the individual's presence. Incidental services, such as typing notes or assisting in entertaining customers, are not enough to warrant a deduction.*

Example: *Jerry drives to Chicago to audition for a play and takes his wife, Linda, with him. Linda is not Jerry's employee. Even if her presence serves a bona fide business purpose, her expenses are not deductible.*

Jerry pays $115 a day for a double room. A single room costs $90 a day. He can deduct the total cost of driving his car to and from Chicago, but only $90 a day for his hotel room. If he uses public transportation, he can deduct only his fare.

Travel Expenses You Can Deduct

This chart summarizes expenses you can deduct when you travel away from home for business purposes.

TABLE 1:

IF you have expenses for:	THEN you can deduct the costs of:
Transportation	Travel by airplane, train, bus, or car between your home and your business destination. If you were provided with a ticket or you are riding free as a result of a frequent traveler or similar program, your cost is zero. If you travel by ship, see additional rules & limits on Luxury Water Travel & Cruise Ships.
Taxi, commuter bus, and airport limousine	Fares for these and other types of transportation that take you to or from: 1) The airport or station and your hotel, and 2) The hotel and the work location of your staff, crew, band members, customers or clients, your business meeting place, or your temporary work location.
Baggage and shipping	Sending baggage, wardrobes, sets & props, sample or display material between your regular and temporary work locations.
Car	Operating and maintaining your car when traveling away from home on business. You can deduct actual expenses or the standard mileage rate, as well as business-related tolls and parking. If you rent a car while away from home on business, you can deduct only the business-use portion of the expenses.
Lodging and meals	Your lodging and meals if your business trip is overnight or long enough that you need to stop for sleep or rest to properly perform your duties. Meals include amounts spent for food, beverage, taxes, and related tips.
Cleaning	Dry cleaning and laundry.
Telephone	Business calls while on your business trip. This includes business communication by fax machine, cellular phone or other communication devices.
Tips	Tips you pay for any expenses in this chart.
Other	Other similar ordinary and necessary expenses related to your business travel. These expenses might include transportation to or from a business meal, public stenographer's fees, computer rental fees, and operating and maintaining a house trailer.

In short, deductible travel is when you are taken away from your home for a direct, clearly identifiable business purpose. Keep in mind: meals are almost always only 50% deductible.

Examples:

On Wednesday Liz Brushstroke drives to NYC to deliver some artwork to the gallery for a new show. The opening is taking place two days later, on Friday. Both Liz and the gallery owner know that it will be good for business if Liz is at the opening, so she stays on in NYC through Friday and drives back on Saturday. This is primarily business; consequently Liz will be able to deduct almost 100% of the costs of the trip. She can either use the IRS per diem rates for meals while in NYC or keep her actual receipts (remember that meals are only 50% deductible).

Guy Focal has a chance to go to Chicago to promote his new children's book at a well-known book fair. The publisher has agreed to pay for his flight to Chicago, but he will have to cover all his expenses while there personally. Guy has a good friend in Chicago who he stays with, so his lodging expenses will be zero. What deductible travel expenses will he have? He will be able to deduct all his meals, taxi fares and other ground transportation; he has some entertainment expenses for taking his publisher out to lunch; and he purchases some other children's books at the show for research purposes, etc.

Use of the IRS Per Diem Rates

The US Government publishes and continually adjusts per diem rates for meals, incidentals and lodging worldwide. Per diem rates for meals and incidentals work a little like the standard mileage allowance discussed earlier. If the artist decides that keeping receipts is too time consuming, he or she can choose to use these standard rates for all their meals and incidentals while traveling in a particular year. The IRS explains the standard rate in its Publication 463:

> *You generally can deduct a standard amount for your daily meals and incidental expenses (M&IE) while you are traveling away from home on business. In this publication, "standard meal allowance" refers to the federal rate for M&IE (which varies based on where and when you travel).*
>
> *Incidental expenses. These include, but are not limited to, your costs for the following items.*
>
> *1) Laundry, cleaning and pressing of clothing.*

2) Fees and tips for persons who provide services, such as porters and baggage carriers.

Incidental expenses do not include taxicab fares, lodging taxes, or the costs of telegrams or telephone calls.

The standard meal allowance method is an alternative to the actual cost method. It allows you to deduct a set amount, depending on where and when you travel, instead of keeping records of your actual costs. If you use the standard meal allowance, you still must keep records to prove the time, place, and business purpose of your travel.

Caution. There is no optional standard lodging amount similar to the standard meal allowance. Your allowable lodging expense deduction is your actual cost.

Who can use the standard meal allowance. You can use the standard meal allowance whether you are an employee or self-employed, and whether or not you are reimbursed for your traveling expenses. You cannot use the standard meal allowance if you are related to your employer.

Use of the standard meal allowance for other travel. You can use the standard meal allowance to prove meal expenses you have when you travel in connection with investment and other income-producing property. You can also use it to prove meal expenses you have when you travel for qualifying educational purposes. You cannot use the standard meal allowance to prove the amount of your meals when you travel for medical or charitable purposes.

Amount of standard meal allowance. The standard meal allowance is the federal M&IE rate. For travel in 2001, the rate is $30 a day for most areas in the United States. Other locations in the United States are designated as high-cost areas, qualifying for higher standard meal allowances. Locations qualifying for rates of $34, $38, $42, or $46 a day are listed in Publication 1542.

If you travel to more than one location in one day, use the rate in effect for the area where you stop for sleep or rest.

50% limit may apply. If you are not reimbursed or if you are reimbursed under a nonaccountable plan for meal expenses, you can generally deduct only 50% of the standard meal allowance. If you are reimbursed under an accountable plan and you are deducting amounts that are more than your reimbursements, you can deduct only 50% of the excess amount.

Standard meal allowance for areas outside the continental United States. The standard meal allowance rates do not apply to travel in Alaska, Hawaii, or any other locations outside the continental United States. The federal per diem rates for these locations are published monthly in the Maximum Travel Per Diem Allowances for Foreign Areas.

The general CONUS (continental US) per diem rate for 2001 is $85 a day. This is allocated as $55 for lodging and $30 for meals and incidentals. Locations deemed to be "high cost" localities, such as New York City, will have higher meals and incidental per diem rates. The US Government also publishes foreign per diem rates OCONUS (outside continental US) to be used for foreign travel. Rates vary from city to city; to get the latest per diem rates obtain Publication 1542 or visit the U.S. General Services Administration Website www.policyworks.gov/perdiem.

Artists can choose to use the meals and incidentals per diem rates for all their business travel in lieu of keeping receipts. Please note: You cannot use a per diem rate for lodging; for that you must always have receipts. If your employer reimburses you using the US Government per diem rates, you may be able to deduct any amount that you spend in excess of the per diem.

A question frequently asked is whether the artist has any tax deductions if the employer covers or reimburses the artist for all expenses. The answer centers on what type of expense plan the employer operates. The IRS allows two basic plans:

1. Accountable Plan — If the employer has what is called an "accountable plan" the artist will typically not have any tax-deductible costs. In this scenario either the artist is reimbursed using the US Government per diem allowances or the artist submits all receipts and details on an expense report (or similar document) and the employer reimburses the artist directly for all the costs. Sometimes the employer may pay a hotel and other things directly. In an accountable plan if all the costs are being covered by the employer, the artist will have not have any tax deductions. What if your employer would have covered a particular expense, but you forgot to submit it, can you deduct the expense? Absolutely not! Say our bassist Sonny Phunky notices, when he is doing his tax returns, that he had forgotten to submit a hotel bill to a band he was employed with during the year. Even when his contract clearly states that all living expenses would be covered (the IRS will review these contracts if they audit him), he will not be able to deduct the bills even if he is past the point of getting reimbursed by the employer. This hotel bill becomes what I call a "tax orphan" that nobody gets to deduct!

2. Non-Accountable Plan — This plan allows the employer simply to give the artist a flat amount in addition to wages on the W–2 to

"cover" expenses. Using this system the artist would be able to deduct all allowable expenses incurred.

Entertainment Expenses

The issue of entertaining, like many others, takes on a different hue for the artist. While some entertaining the artist might do is clear-cut as business related, such as meeting with his or her agent over lunch, a lot of entertaining which the artist considers "business related," the IRS views with suspicion. Before looking at specific examples of business entertainment, let's see how the IRS views the subject in their Publication 463:

> ### General rule:
> *You can deduct ordinary and necessary expenses to entertain a client, customer, or employee if the expenses meet the directly related test or the associated test.*
>
> ### Definitions:
> ✓ *Entertainment includes any activity generally considered to provide entertainment, amusement, or recreation, and includes meals provided to a customer or client.*
> ✓ *An ordinary expense is one that is common and accepted in your field of business, trade, or profession.*
> ✓ *A necessary expense is one that is helpful and appropriate, although not necessarily indispensable, for your business.*
>
> ### Tests to be meet the directly related test:
> ✓ *Entertainment took place in a clear business setting, or*
> ✓ *Main purpose of entertainment was the active conduct of business, and*
> ✓ *You did engage in business with the person during the entertainment period, and*
> ✓ *You had more than a general expectation of getting income or some other specific business benefit.*
>
> ### Associated test
> ✓ *Entertainment is associated with your trade or business, and*
> ✓ *Entertainment directly precedes or follows a substantial business discussion*
>
> ### Other rules
> ✓ *You cannot deduct the cost of your meal as an entertainment expense if you are claiming the meal as a travel expense.*
> ✓ *You cannot deduct expenses that are lavish or extravagant under the circumstances.*

✓ *You generally can deduct only 50% of your unreimbursed entertainment expenses.*

You can see the IRS takes a hard line view on business entertainment (no surprise there!). It is up to the artist to keep the kind of records necessary to support the deduction. Interestingly, although the IRS does not require a receipt if the cost of the entertainment is less then $75, they are sure going to ask for substantiation. Your main friend here will be a detailed diary in your schedule book that lists of who was present, what business matters were discussed and where the event was held.

Substantiating Your Deductions for Travel, Meals & Entertainment

The area of travel, meals & entertainment presents difficult substantiation issues for the artist. It is easy to keep records when you pay your business phone, buy a professional book or magazine, pay an agent, etc., but when you take a potential employer, buyer, agent, publisher, producer or colleague out to lunch, how do you "account" for that? What will the IRS ask for to substantiate your travel, meals & entertainment deductions? You will need two types of records in case the IRS comes knocking:

1. A diary, account book, calendar, schedule book. If you use one of the popular electronic PDAs (Personal Digital Assistants) print out a hard copy of your schedule or back it up to the hard drive of your computer. Record the details of the travel, entertainment and meal, including time, place, who was present, and the business purpose.
2. Receipts and itemized bills for meals and entertainment instances under $75 don't require a receipt (an entry in your diary will do), lodging, meals and entertainment OVER $75 do. For these costs keep all receipts and itemized bills.

Here are the exceptions (you knew they were coming!):

1. Receipts for transportation expense of $75 or more are required only when they are readily obtainable. This is in response to our era of "ticketless" travel. In which case, if you do have a boarding pass or receipt, keep it.
2. A canceled check or credit card statement is usually not considered adequate in and of itself, though many IRS agents will accept them as corroborating evidence. If you cannot provide a bill, receipt or voucher, you can use other evidence such as written statements from witnesses.

Receipts should show the following:

✓ Amount of expense

✓ Date of expense
✓ Where the expense occurred

In addition to the above information that would typically be preprinted on most receipts, the artist should get into the habit of writing the "who, why and where" directly on the receipts or in their diary/schedule book. For a meal or entertainment expense jot down:

1. *Who* was there
2. *Why* they were there—what the business purpose was and be as specific as possible!
3. *Where* the event was—was it in an atmosphere conducive to business discussions?

The IRS always wants itemized receipts of such things as hotel bills in order to ferret out personal items such as phone calls, gift purchases and movie rentals that may be lurking on the bill.

Are there excuses for NOT having adequate records?

1. Substantial Compliance — If you have made a good faith effort to comply with IRS requirements, you will not be penalized if you do not satisfy every requirement. In other words, missing one or two receipts or forgetting to make notes on a few meals receipts will not necessarily be grounds for the IRS to throw out an expense.
2. Accidental Destruction of Records — House fire, flood, mudslides or other circumstances beyond your control cause your records to be destroyed. In this situation you are allowed to reasonably reconstruct your deductions.
3. Exceptional Circumstances — I doubt if anyone knows what the heck this means; the IRS certainly doesn't explain it in its regulations. The IRS states that if due to the "inherent nature of the situation" you are unable to keep receipts or records you may present alternative evidence.

The "QPA" – Qualified Performing Artist

The concept of the QPA entered the tax code during the tax act of 1986. In that act many, many deductions were completely abolished or diminished by moving them around on the return. One such move was the Form 2106 used to deduct employee business expenses. Prior to 1986 the 2106 was a very common form quite logically used to take employee business deductions directly on the front page of the 1040, with no need to itemize. In 1986 the 2106 was moved from the front page of the 1040 and became an itemized deduction on Schedule A. Not only that; it was now subject to a dreaded 2% floor!

This means that you automatically lose part of your deductions; the amount that is equal to 2% of your adjusted gross income. Due in part to the work of Actors' Equity Association and of Stage Source, among others, a provision was installed in the code of 1986 for what is termed the Qualified Performing Artist. The IRS explains the QPA this way in its Publication 529:

> *If you are a qualified performing artist, you can deduct your employee business expenses as an adjustment to income rather than as a miscellaneous itemized deduction. To qualify, you must meet all three of the following requirements.*
>
> 1. *You perform services in the performing arts for at least two employers during your tax year. (You are considered to have performed services in the performing arts for an employer only if that employer paid you $200 or more.)*
> 2. *Your related performing-arts business expenses are more than 10% of your gross income from the performance of such services.*
> 3. *Your adjusted gross income is not more than $16,000 before deducting these business expenses.*
>
> *If you do not meet all of the above requirements, you must deduct your expenses as a miscellaneous itemized deduction on schedule A subject to the 2% limit.*
>
> **Special rules for married persons**. *If you are married, you must file a joint return unless you lived apart from your spouse at all times during the tax year.*
>
> *If you file a joint return, you must figure requirements (1) and (2) above separately for both you and your spouse. However, requirement (3) applies to your and your spouse's combined adjusted gross income.*
>
> **Where to report**. *If you meet all of the above requirements, you should first complete Form 2106 or Form 2106–EZ. Then you include your performing-arts related expenses from line 10 of Form 2106 or from line 6 of Form 2106–EZ on line 32 of Form 1040. Then write "QPA" and the amount of your performing-arts related expenses on the dotted line next to line 32 (Form 1040).*

There has been great consternation regarding the fact that the QPA is so limited. These thresholds have NEVER been increased since the measure was adopted in 1986! So, the QPA provision is useful to fewer and fewer folks each year, but it is still a great tax benefit for those who can use it.

The "Hobby Loss" Issue

When you begin your career in the arts, it is quite likely that your expenses will exceed your income resulting in a loss on your tax return. When this happens in succeeding years you have the potential for the IRS to declare your career as an artist "a hobby." How does the IRS deem an activity to be a hobby (something "not engaged in for profit" to use its terminology)? This is how it is explained in the Publication 535:

> *If you do not carry on your business or investment activity to make a profit, there is a limit on the deductions you can take. You cannot use a loss from the activity to offset other income. Activities you do as a hobby, or mainly for sport or recreation, come under this limit. So does an investment activity intended only to produce tax losses for the investors.*
>
> *The limit on not-for-profit losses applies to individuals, partnerships, estates, trusts, and S corporations. It does not apply to corporations other than S corporations.*
>
> *In determining whether you are carrying on an activity for profit, all the facts are taken into account. No one factor alone is decisive. Among the factors to consider are whether:*
>
> 1. *You carry on the activity in a businesslike manner,*
> 2. *The time and effort you put into the activity indicate you intend to make it profitable,*
> 3. *You depend on income from the activity for your livelihood,*
> 4. *Your losses are due to circumstances beyond your control (or are normal in the start-up phase of your type of business),*
> 5. *You change your methods of operation in an attempt to improve profitability,*
> 6. *You, or your advisors, have the knowledge needed to carry on the activity as a successful business,*
> 7. *You were successful in making a profit in similar activities in the past,*
> 8. *The activity makes a profit in some years, and how much profit it makes, and*
> 9. *You can expect to make a future profit from the appreciation of the assets used in the activity.*

Many things that one would consider a "hobby" are obvious. Examples would be, the attorney who attempts to take his stamp collecting and turn it into a business, thus creating a tax-deductible loss, or the doctor who tries to write off his horse-breeding hobby as a business. Unfortunately, the IRS has established a codified "test" for deciding what is a hobby. This "presumption of profit" test below is from Publication 535:

> *An activity is presumed carried on for profit if it produced a profit in at least 3 of the last 5 tax years, including the current year. You have a profit when the gross income from an activity is more than the deductions for it.*
>
> *If a taxpayer dies before the end of the 5-year period, the period ends on the date of the taxpayer's death.*
>
> *If your business or investment activity passes this 3-years-of-profit test, presume it is carried on for profit. This means it will not come under these limits. You can take all your business deductions from the activity, even for the years that you have a loss. You can rely on this presumption in every case, unless the IRS shows it is not valid.*
>
> *Using the presumption later. If you are starting an activity and do not have 3 years showing a profit, you may want to take advantage of this presumption later, after you have the 5 years of experience allowed by the test.*
>
> *You can choose to do this by filing Form 5213. Filing this form postpones any determination that your activity is not carried on for profit until 5 years have passed since you started the activity.*
>
> *The benefit gained by making this choice is that the IRS will not immediately question whether your activity is engaged in for profit. Accordingly, it will not restrict your deductions. Rather, you will gain time to earn a profit in 3 out of the first 5 years you carry on the activity. If you show 3 years of profit at the end of this period, your deductions are not limited under these rules. If you do not have 3 years of profit, the limit can be applied retroactively to any year in the 5-year period with a loss.*
>
> *Filing Form 5213 automatically extends the period of limitations on any year in the 5-year period to 2 years after the due date of the return for the last year of the period. The period is extended only for deductions of the activity and any related deductions that might be affected.*

This "hobby loss" is an audit trap that you do not want to land in, as it can be very expensive. The IRS is not automatically tracking this deduction through its computer (at least not yet) and is only likely to come up in an audit situation when the agent has the opportunity, or reason, to look at several consecutive years of returns. Are artists dead in the water if they have had three consecutive years of losses? Not necessarily. The Second Circuit Court said in a decision issued in 1995: "Code section 183 [the section where the "hobby loss" provisions live] isn't designed to punish the inept only those who deliberately engage in unprofitable activities and with a view to sheltering income." There are numerous instances where the tax court has allowed folks to write off continual losses, against the wishes of the IRS, but be prepared for a fight. Complete and detailed records of your ongoing activities can make a huge difference.

To me the hobby loss area is where you see the palpable difference between the person who opens a local hardware store and the one who is the artist. That is because success is obviously and historically far more elusive for the artist than it is for a retail store owner. When Fred opens his corner hardware store he will quickly close it if he is not making money. Whereas folks in the arts will often go on for years racking up losses searching for that "big break."

Unfortunately again for us, when this issue rears its head the IRS agent views the artist and Fred's Corner Hardware store in exactly the same light. In the same way he or she examines Fred's hardware store, the IRS agent will look at your career in the arts as strictly a business proposition, and you will need to clearly prove that you have a profit motive. The heart of this matter is that you have to show that you are attempting to ***make money***. It's that simple. Your records need to show clearly a concerted, consistent, ongoing, business like effort to land the next acting job, sell the article, publish the new book, get the gig, land the recording contract and sell the artwork. Your career in the arts needs to have all the attributes of a business in every sense of the word.

Start-up Costs

If you are new to your profession as an artist you may initially incur what the IRS calls start-up costs. Start up costs are legitimate deductible expense that occur before the business has actually started, an example being a writer who spends the first two years of a career writing his or her first book. Since no manuscripts were produced and, more importantly, no marketing of any of the author's works was undertaken, all the deductions from the first two years would be deemed by the IRS to be startup costs. If you have start-up costs, the expenses are added together and then written off (*amortized*) over 3 years.

In closing . . .

We have looked at some of the larger expense issues and have seen how the IRS views these matters by looking at their publications. Now let us move on to more specific applications. In the next four chapters we will visit in turn our four artists in residence and see how all this information plays out in each of their returns.

3

For Actors, Directors, Dancers and Other Show Biz Folks Only

In this chapter I will look in detail at the activities of our good friend Ima Starr and the kind of income and deductions she had for the year.

First, let's walk through some of the expense items for show biz folks specifically. I will also note in parentheses the type of record keeping the IRS would require:

1. Union dues, professional societies and organizations (invoices & checks)
2. Professional fees for agents, attorneys & accountants (invoices & checks)
3. Professional registries (both printed and on the Internet) including Players Guide, Academy Players, Role Call, Funny Face, etc. (invoices & checks)
4. Classes and coaching lessons (invoices & checks)
5. Cosmetics and dressing room supplies – This does not include street makeup, or what you use going to auditions, but does include makeup for showcases. The IRS can be very aggressive on makeup, so write the name of the show the makeup was used for on the back of the receipt (sales receipts, invoices, credit card receipt & checks)
6. Hair care – This must be for a specific job, not general, looking-for-work upkeep. I recommend that if a director wants you to change hairstyle or color and is not going to pay for it, ask to have a rider put into your contract stating this fact (sales receipts, invoice, credit card receipt & checks)
7. Photographs and resumes – including videos, CDs, CD-ROMs, DVDs and digital image transfers for use on the Internet or your personal Website (sales receipts, invoices, credit card receipt & checks)
8. Stationery and postage (sales receipts & checks)

9. Theatre & film books, scripts, musical scores, sheet music, batteries, tapes, CDs, etc. – these fall under the heading of supplies and may need to be allocated between employment income and contract income (sales receipts, invoices, credit card receipt & checks)

10. Telephone and cellular phone – actual business calls on your home phone are deductible, but the IRS does not allow the allocation of the base monthly rate. You can deduct only the actual long distance charges. The same rule is true with your cellular phone service. If you get a second phone line strictly for business then it can be considered 100% deductible (bills & checks)

11. Wardrobe – This is professional wardrobe not conventional street wear! The rule says if you can wear it on the street, you can't deduct it. Remember that if the wardrobe is deductible then the cleaning is as well. Write in the back of the bill the name of the show that the wardrobe was used in (sales receipts, invoices, credit card receipt & checks)

12. Viewing theatre, films, and concerts (live and via DVD, video and cable) – I often call this expense line item "research"; others refer to it as "performance audit." Whatever you call it, make sure to allocate some of this expense to personal use. After all you must sometimes take part in these activities for personal enjoyment, it can't be all business. I quote to clients the old Wall Street saying, "the pigs get fat and the hogs get slaughtered." This is the type of deduction that you must not get piggy with. While the IRS typically hates this deduction, it does clearly acknowledge its validity in its audit guidelines. In an audit you would need to explain specifically what the professional value was (ticket stubs, receipts & diary entries)

13. Promotional tickets – Only your ticket is deductible, not your date's. That is unless your date is your agent, a producer or some other professional colleague (ticket stubs, receipts & diary entries)

14. Rehearsal hall rental - (invoices & check)

15. Accompanist, arranger, personal assistant, etc. – This person must have a defined business purpose. For instance if your assistant is paying your personal bills or engaging in non-business activities, it will not be deductible (bills, invoices & check)

16. Office rent – you must be able to prove you need one (bills, invoices & checks)

17. Purchase of equipment Computers & printers, cameras, video and sound equipment, etc. (bills, invoices & credit card receipt)

18. Repair of equipment used in your profession - Computers, musical instruments, sound & video equipment, cameras, etc. (bills, credit card receipts, invoices & checks)

19. Tax preparation, bookkeeping & accounting fees (bills, invoices & checks)
20. Demo tapes, videos, DVDs & commercial prints used in promotional activities (bills, invoices & checks)
21. Trade advertisements (bills, invoices, checks & credit card receipt)
22. Internet service – for research purposes, business e-mail and e-mail while on the road. Be sure to allocate some of the costs for personal use (bills, invoices & credit card receipt)
23. Trade papers and professional magazines (bills, invoices, checks & credit card receipt)
24. Backstage tips – Remember you cannot give these folks gifts (checks & diary entry)
25. Insurance (bills, invoices & checks)
26. Copyright Fees (invoices & checks)

We already know our resident actor Ima has been very busy. She is a member of Actors' Equity and received multiple W–2s this year for her work in theatre and films. She was also a part time singer in the group The Blue Jazzbos. She had even found the time to do some modeling, and she had finally finished her book, one of those kiss-and-tell books about her life in show business.

We'll review some of Ima's employment (W–2) income. In Chapter 1 we saw her W–2 from the Goodwrench Theatre in Philadelphia for her work in *Godspell*. We find out the Goodwrench is barely surviving so it could not offer her any expense reimbursements. This means that Ima can deduct virtually all her costs while staying in Philadelphia. These include meals, using the Philadelphia per diem rate of $42, actual hotel accommodations, clothes cleaning, telephone calls home. She can also deduct any professional costs associated with the show, wardrobe (if unsuited for street wear), scripts, etc.

Ima's next gig was a great job in California: a small part in a movie starring Mel Fun. Mel's production company Way Down Under Productions, Inc., employed her. Since The company paid all her transportation and living expenses she would have no deductions for those. (Both Actors' Equity and SAG operate "Accountable Plans" as far as expense reimbursements are concerned, which means that Ima's reimbursements will not usually appear on her W–2.) To prepare for her role she rented DVDs of all of Mr. Fun's movies and purchased a book about his life. She bought a new DVD player that together with these expenses would all be deductible as research on her Form 2106 (employee business expense). The DVD player will be depreciated over 5 years, or she could use the Section 179 election and write it all off this year. She may choose to allocate some of the DVD cost as personal expenses and write off only a percentage of the player. To do further research into the Mr. Fun's career Ima used her Internet service, making part of her Internet service deductible.

On the strength of some of the connections Ima made in California during the above-mentioned gig she made a second trip to California. Ima wanted to be certain the trip would be 100% deductible, so she set up appointments in advance and consulted *Variety* to see what open auditions and productions would be taking place during her stay. She needed to ensure she had enough daily activity to show the IRS that the trip was primarily business. During her six-day stay in California Ima set up lunch appointments almost every day with various industry types who had job potential for her. She arranged in advance an appointment with folks in Mel Fun's production company regarding other potential film assignments. While in California Ima stayed with a friend at no cost to her. She ate with her friend, again at no charge when she was not combining business meetings with meals. Ima will be able to deduct her travel, taxi (or rental car), etc., as business related, and her meals with the industry types as business entertainment deductions. Ima dutifully wrote the "who, what, & where" of each meal in her electronic organizer which she later printed out to retain a hard copy for her permanent record. Indeed, she made notes in her organizer regarding all her business activity while in LA. By doing her homework and planning her trip in advance she had made it far more likely that an IRS agent would consider the trip a legitimate business deduction. What if Ima did not have a friend in LA to stay with, would she be able to deduct her hotel and non-entertainment meals while there? Absolutely yes!

As a result of this second visit to California Ima got a part in a movie playing a famous woman aviator of the 1940s. To prepare for the role she searched the Internet and located an individual who owned a plane similar to the one this famous flyer would have flown. She offered to pay the plane's owner to take her flying and help give her a feel for the plane. This individual did not charge her, but she did have to travel some distance to meet with him. Because this research was for a particular role and had a clear, well-defined purpose all the costs associated with this trip will be fully deductible. Ima will need to have some evidence of the trip, such as a letter from the plane's owner or perhaps a photograph of her with the plane.

During the summer Ima landed some summer stock work on Cape Cod. The theatre offers no monetary reimbursement provides the players a place to live while there. Ima would have expenses for meals and incidentals, but obviously not for lodging. Ima uses the IRS per diem rates for all her meals and incidentals throughout the year. The daily rate for Martha's Vineyard on Cape Cod, MA (a designated high cost locality), is $42 a day for 2001. Of course, her mileage driving to the Cape, including the ferry, and auto use while there would be deductible.

In late summer Ima had a chance to audition for a musical being staged in London's West End. She flew to London for the audition, and then decided to stay on for several weeks for a vacation. Her agent had arranged for her to meet with other theatre and film folk while there. She and her accountant decided that she had spent about 30% of her time on clearly defined business related activities. These activities included appointments with agents, casting directors, and other actors. She had kept business cards and made notes in her schedule book regarding each meeting so that she had records backing up the business purpose. To gauge what the British theatre scene was like she attended some performances. The IRS might balk at these theatre ticket expenses, but Ima figures it is worth a try. She kept all the ticket stubs and noted the business reason in her diary. Because the trip was outside the US and more than 25% of the trip was personal, Ima will prorate the trip's costs taking 30% only as a business expense.

Next Ima goes on a tour singing with The Blue Jazzbos. It was a southern tour with no expenses reimbursed. Ima decided to purchase a new sound system and microphone, as the one she had been using was no longer adequate and she was not sure if the clubs would have a PA system. The income from the tour will be reported on Ima's schedule C because it is self-employment income. The depreciation for the sound system and microphone will be written off over 5 years and deducted on her Schedule C, as will all her travel expenses. To help her work up a Peggy Lee medley for the tour Ima purchases a new box set of CDs by Ms. Lee; this will become another expense on her Schedule C. Ima also took a few lessons, which are tax deductible, from a noted New York singer in regards to matters of stage presence. The leader of the Jazzbos wanted the band members to get new formal wear for the tour. As you know for clothing to be deductible it has to be:

1. Required to keep your job;
2. Not suitable for wear when not working

Ima bought an evening gown expressly for this tour. This is not a clear-cut deduction, but the IRS has allowed the deduction of formal wear for musicians. If Ima can deduct the clothing, she can also deduct the cleaning of the gown. The band members will also have some income from selling copies of their self-produced CD. Copies of the CD that Ima purchases to sell will become a "cost of goods sold" on her Schedule C.

Back in New York, Ima did a series of small modeling assignments. These were all paid as contract income and other than some mileage expenses going between jobs she did not have any direct expenses. This income was reported on Schedule C and Ima allocated some of her home office expense to it using the gross income method discussed in Chapter 2.

Because Ima is fairly well known in NYC she had a unique opportunity to endorse a well-known local brand of pizza during the year. The small pizzeria chain starred Ima in its local cable TV ad. In addition to her pay, she received free pizza for a year. At the end of the year the pizzeria chain estimated that Ima had received about $550 worth of pizza. Ima declared the $550 value of the pizza as self-employment income on her tax return.

Ima received her first advance royalty income from her book in December. This income will be reported on her Schedule C. She had allocated some expenses for her home office, computer, printer, office supplies, Internet use, etc. She added the expense of a writing class she had taken at Columbia University earlier in the year while she was finishing her book. For the Columbia class Ima has the choice of using the Lifetime Learning credit or taking the expense as a deduction on her Schedule C form. Her accountant will calculate it both ways to see what yields the most tax benefit. She included some research expense, as she had purchased and read some other famous Hollywood and theatre memoirs. In May, as she was finishing her book, she flew out to California to visit with a colleague to check on the accuracy some incidents she had used. She was in LA for two days interviewing her friend. The entire costs of this trip would be deductible against her book income.

Ima decided that she wanted to set up a personal Website, where she could post her resume, pictures, some sound clips of her singing from The Blue Jazzbos CD and perhaps some video clips from performances. The costs of setting up the Website, registering her domain name and hosting the site will all be deductible. The IRS stipulates that Website development be written-off (amortized) over 3 years. So all the costs of setting up and designing the site will be added up (capitalized) and expensed over 3 years.

In the fall Ima decided to purchase some video equipment to experiment with filmmaking and allow her to shoot her own promotional videos. Because it is directly related to her career, the cost of the equipment will be deductible. She did not have the cash to purchase the equipment outright, so she charged it on her credit card and is paying a little off each month. The full cost of the equipment will be deductible in the current year and will be depreciated over 5 years.

Near the end of the year, an audition opportunity in Chicago came up. Ima arrived in Chicago on Monday evening and had her audition on Tuesday morning. She waited in town to hear back from the director on Wednesday. On Wednesday afternoon she received a callback, and met with the director again on Thursday morning. After the callback, she decided to stay on and visit with a friend for a few days; she returned to NYC on Sunday. She can clearly show that a preponderance of time was spent in directly related business activities. Therefore 100% of her airline travel expenses to Chicago would be deductible. Her other expenses, such as hotel, meals and incidentals, would be fully deductible through Thursday (the day the business part of the trip ended). The meals & lodging expenses while she was visiting her friend would not be deductible. FYI: If the scales tip the other way and the trip begins to be more personal than business none of the travel expense is deductible.

Ima is considering moving to California and calls her accountant to ask him or her if the move would be deductible. She finds out that she has two main criteria to meet. The first concerns distance, the second relates to time. Here are the details from IRS Publication 521:

1. *Your move will meet the distance test if your new main job location is at least 50 miles farther from your former home than your old main job location was from your former home. For example, if your old job was 3 miles from your former home, your new job must be at least 53 miles from that former home.*

2. *If you are an employee, you must work full time for at least 39 weeks during the first 12 months after you arrive in the general area of your new job location. For this time test, count only your full-time work as an employee; do not count any work you do as a self-employed person. You do not have to work for the same employer for the 39 weeks. You do not have to work 39 weeks in a row. However, you must work full time within the same general commuting area. Full-time employment depends on what is usual for your type of work in your area.*

The moving deduction can be a difficult issue for folks in the arts such as Ima. Employment and income is often not consistent thus making it hard to meet the 39 week rule. The key phrase to focus on is: *"employment depends on what is usual for your type of work in your area."* Ima will have to be ready to argue that her employment and work circumstances were typical for her acting, singing and modeling jobs.

If she thinks she will have a tax-deductible move she will be saving receipts for the following costs according to the IRS Publication 521:

1. *Moving your household goods and personal effects (including in-transit storage expenses), and*
2. *Traveling (including lodging but not meals) to your new home.*

Internet Resources for Actors, Directors, Dancers and Other Show Biz Folk

The Internet has become a tremendous source of information for actors and other show biz folk—these are some of the Websites I have found useful:

The first, of course, is the official Website of this very book—www.arts-tax-info.com—there you can print and download various checklists, worksheets and links to the Websites listed below and get updates on all the latest tax changes that affect actors and other show biz folk.

www.backstage.com – Complete Online Performing Arts Website

www.magicmagazine.com – Independent Magazine for Magicians
www.playbill.com – Playbill Magazine Online
www.stage-directions.com – Stage Directions Magazine
www.stagebill.com – Stagebill
www.showbusinessweekly.com – Show Business Online
www.curtainup.com – The Internet Theatre Magazine of News and Reviews
www.dancemagazine.com – Dance Magazine
www.danceronline.com – Dancer Online
www.pointemagazine.com – Pointe Magazine, Ballet at its Best
www.allmovie.com – The great All Movie Guide on the Web
www.aftra.org – The American Federation of Television and Radio Artists
www.actorsequity.org – Actors' Equity Association
www.dga.org – Directors Guild of America
www.onstage.org – Onstage, The Performers Resource
www.sag.com – Screen Actors Guild
www.filmmag.com – Filmmaker Magazine
www.billboardtalentnet.com – Billboard Talent Net
www.ascap.org – American Society of Composers, Authors & Publishers
www.wga.org – Writers Guild of America
www.variety.com – Variety Magazine
www.backstagecasting.com – Backstage Magazine
www.bmi.com – Broadcast Music, Inc.
www.vcu.edu/artweb/playwriting – The Dramatists Guild
www.macnyc.com – Manhattan Association of Cabarets & Clubs
www.hollywoodreporter.com – The Hollywood Reporter
www.hcdonline.com – Hollywood Creative Directory
www.ifp.org – Independent Feature Project
www.emmyonline.org – National Academy of Television Arts & Sciences
www.mpaa.org – Motion Picture Association of America
www.oscars.org – Academy of Motion Picture Arts & Sciences
www.afionline.org – The American Film Institute
www.refdeck.com – The single best source of facts on the Internet
www.lcweb.loc.gov/copyright – The US Government Copyright Office
www.writersdigest.com – Writers Digest
www.taxresources.com/ – The Internets best single source of tax related links
www.irs.gov – The Internal Revenue Service
www.info.gov – FCIC National Contact Center – Portal to US Government
    information
www.switchboard.com/ – Find people, get directions, etc.
www.yahoo.com – Huge portal to all sorts of information, get a personal e-
    mail account and directions anywhere in the country

Actors, Directors, & other Performing Artists

Continuing Education		Auto Travel (in miles)	
Coaching & Lessons		Auditions	
Dance Training		Business Meetings	
Music - Arrangements		Continuing Education	
Tapes, CDs & Recordings		Job Seeking	
Training		Out-Of-Town Business Trips	
Rents - Rehearsal Hall		Purchasing Job Supplies & Materials	
Tickets - Performance Audit/Research		Professional Society Meetings	
Voice Training		Parking Fees & Tolls	
Other: _____		Other:_____	

Promotional Expenses		Travel - Out of Town	
Audition Tapes, Videos & DVDs		Airfare	
Business Cards		Car Rental	
Film & Processing		Parking	
Mailing Supplies - Envelopes, etc.		Taxi, Train, Bus & Subway	
Photos - Professional		Lodging (do not combine with meals)	
Website Development & Hosting		Apartment Rent (jobs lasting less than 1 year)	
Resume and Portfolio Expenses		Meals (do not combine with lodging)	
Other:_____		Laundry and Porter	
Supplies & Other Expenses		Bridge & Highway Tolls	
Alterations/Repairs (costumes)		Telephone Calls (including home)	
Cleaning (costumes/wardrobe)		Other:_____	
Costumes - Wardrobe (special business)		**Telephone Costs**	
Dues - Union & Professional		Cellular Calls	
Gifts - Business ($25 maximum per person per year)		FAX Transmissions	
		Online Services	
Insurance - Equipment		Paging Service	
Interest - Business Loans		Pay Phone	
Makeup - Cosmetics (special business)		Toll Calls	
Manicure - (special for hand inserts)		Other:_____	
Meals - Business (100% of cost)		**Equipment Purchases**	
Photocopy - Scripts, etc.		Answering Machine	
Postage & Office Supplies		Personal Digital Assistants (PDAs)	
Props, Stunt Supplies		Audio Systems	
Publications - Trade		Musical Instruments	
Rents - Office, Storage, etc.		Pager and Recorder	
Rents - Equipment, Costumes, etc.		Camera & Video Equipment	
Repairs - Equipment		Speaker Systems	
Secretarial & Bookkeeping		Computers, Software & Printers	
Commissions - Agent/Manager		Office Furniture	
Other: _____		Other: _____	

4

For Musicians
and Singers Only

In this chapter I will look in detail at the activities of our good friend Sonny Phunky and the kind of income and deductions he had for the year.

To begin, we'll walk through some of the expense items for musicians and singers specifically. I will note in parentheses the type of record keeping the IRS would require:

1. Union dues and professional societies (invoices & checks)
2. Professional fees for agents, attorneys & accountants (invoices & checks)
3. Professional registries – (both printed and on the Internet) (invoices, credit card receipt & checks)
4. Master classes, education and coaching lessons (invoices & checks)
5. Stage makeup - This does not include street makeup, or what you use going to auditions, but does include makeup for showcases. The IRS can be very aggressive on makeup so write the name of the gig the makeup was used for on the back of the receipt (invoices, credit card receipt & checks)
6. Hair care – This must be a particular style for a specific gig, not general, looking-for-work upkeep (sales receipts, credit card receipt & checks)
7. Photographs and resumes – including videos, CDs, CD-ROMs, DVDs and digital image transfers for use on the Internet or your personal Website (sales receipts, credit card receipt & checks)
8. Stationery and postage (sales receipts & checks)
9. Music books, musical scores, sheet music, batteries, tapes, CDs, etc – these fall under the heading of supplies and may need to be allocated between employment income and contract income (invoices, credit card receipt & checks)
10. Telephone and cellular phone – actual business calls on your home phone are deductible, but the IRS does not allow the allocation of the base monthly rate. You can deduct only the actual long distance

charges. The same rule is true with your cellular phone service. If you get a second phone line strictly for business then it can be considered 100% deductible (bills & checks)

11. Internet service – for research purposes, business e-mail and e-mail while on the road. Be sure to allocate some of the costs for personal use (bills, invoice & credit card receipt)

12. Stage clothes – This is professional uniforms, not conventional street wear! The rule says if you can wear it on the street, you can't deduct it. Remember that if the uniform is deductible then the cleaning is as well. A special rule allows musicians to deduct purchase of formal wear (invoices, credit card receipt & checks)

13. Viewing concerts, performances and films (live and via DVD, video and cable) – I often call this expense line item "research"; others refer to it as "performance audit." Whatever you call it, make sure to allocate some of this expense to personal use. After all you must sometimes take part in these activities for personal enjoyment, it can't be all business. I often quote to clients the old Wall Street saying, "the pigs get fat and the hogs get slaughtered." This is the type of deduction that you must not get piggy with. While the IRS typically hates this deduction, it does clearly acknowledge its validity in its audit guidelines. In an audit you would need to explain specifically what the professional value was (ticket stubs, receipts & diary entries)

14. Promotional tickets – Only your ticket is deductible, not your date's, unless your date is your agent a band member, producer or some other professional colleague (ticket stubs, receipts & diary entries)

15. Rehearsal hall or club rental - (invoices & checks)

16. Accompanist, arranger, sideman, sound or lighting person, personal assistant, etc. – This person must have a defined business purpose. For instance, if your personal assistant is paying your personal bills or engaged in non-business activities, it will not be deductible. Also if any of these folks are contractors and they receive more than $600 in a calendar year you must issue them a form 1099–MISC (invoices & checks)

17. Office rent – you must be able to prove you need an outside office (bills, invoices & checks)

18. Repair of equipment – Computers, musical instruments, sound & video equipment (bills, invoices, credit card receipt & checks)

19. Tax preparation, bookkeeping & accounting fees (bills, invoices & checks)

20. Demo tapes, videos, DVDs & commercial prints – Used in promotional activities (bills, invoices & checks)

21. Trade advertisements (invoices, credit card receipt & checks)

22. Trade papers and professional magazines (invoices, credit card receipt & checks)
23. Backstage tips – Note: you cannot give these folks gifts (checks & diary entry)
24. Insurance – Including riders on your home insurance policy to cover home studio or other business activities (bills, invoices & checks)
25. Copyright fees (invoices & checks)
26. Equipment Purchases – Sound equipment, instruments, etc. (bills, invoices, credit card receipt & checks)

Now, let's see what kind of year our bass player Sonny Phunky had.

You'll recall that Sonny was hired to play on a national tour with the Butterball Kings rock band. Let's look at some of the expenses that Sonny incurred during this time. Sonny lives in Maine so he had to travel to New York City, where the band rehearsed prior to beginning their tour. Sonny rehearsed with the Butterball Kings for three weeks in New York City. Sonny was paid a per diem that was higher then the IRS approved rate (as you will remember from Chapter 1 when we analyzed Sonny's W–2 from his work with the Butterball Kings.) The excess $1,176 was reported as taxable wages in box 1 on Sonny's W–2. In other words, Sonny has to pay taxes on the excess per diem paid to him above the amount that the IRS allows. Fortunately Sonny had the receipts to support the additional deduction, so he was able to write-off living expenses to offset the extra $1,176 that was reported as W–2 income. Sonny had depreciation expenses for the new chartreuse colored bass he purchased specifically for this gig. During the NYC rehearsal period, Sonny had expenses for supplies, such as new strings, cords and music books. He purchased a variety of CDs in order to learn some of the music the band played and he had a local repair shop overhaul his bass amplifier so that it was in good working order for the tour. Sonny used all these above expenses as deductions against the W–2.

In anticipation of the money he was going to earn on his gig with the Butterball Kings he splurged almost $10,000 on a rare 1954 Fender® Telecaster® electric bass guitar. His accountant felt that the rare antique instrument might not be deductible until Sonny told him that he had used it on several studio dates and gigs during the year. The fact that this guitar was used in his profession (as opposed to being primarily a collectable piece) will probably make the purchase deductible. His tax advisor told Sonny to get some pictures of him using the guitar in the studio and on stage, in case he was audited. Because Sonny used the guitar on jobs that were mainly contract income, his accountant depreciated the guitar over 7 years as a write-off on Sonny's Schedule C.

During the summer Sonny landed a gig playing for a popular show band in Atlantic City. The band did not offer any monetary reimbursement but gave the players a place to live there. In this case, Sonny had expenses for meals and incidentals, but obviously not for lodging. Sonny is a terrible record keeper and uses the IRS per diem rates for all his meals and incidentals throughout the year. The daily rate for Atlantic City is $30 a day for 2001. Of course, his mileage driving to New Jersey and auto use while there were deductible.

In July Sonny went to the NAMM (International Association of Music Merchandisers) trade show. A luthier who he knows asked him to appear in his exhibition booth to endorse and demonstrate a new bass guitar he had designed. The luthier could not pay cash to Sonny for the appearance, so he gave him one of his handmade basses worth an estimated $2,000. The trip did give Sonny a chance to see new products at the show, hand his card and CD out to recordings studios and generally network with other industry and music types. He attended the show for the entire three days he was gone. Sonny could clearly show a business purpose and was able to deduct the entire trip. He will declare the $2,000 value of the bass as self-employment income on his Schedule C.

When Sonny is not away from home on gigs he has a standing weekend job at a local bar in Rockridge, Maine. His band, The Over the Hill Gang is an impromptu one made up of whoever is available that night. The club owner pays Sonny and Sonny in turn pays the band. The club owner issued Sonny a 1099–MISC at the end of the year that included all the funds he had paid Sonny over the year for his band. Sonny then went through his records to obtain a list of all the sidemen he had paid $600 or more to in the year. He ended up issuing five 1099–MISC forms to these musicians. To issue a 1099–MISC, Sonny needed the musician's full name, address and social security number. Sonny's accountant had alerted him to this requirement, so Sonny had all his musicians fill out the federal form W-9 to ensure he would be sure to have all this information at year-end. His accountant gave Sonny a pile of W-9 Forms to keep in his guitar case. Of course all the sidemen he had paid during the year were deductions against his income on his Schedule C form, even those that made less than $600.

Sonny had one particularly good combination of his The Over the Hill Gang during the year, which he was able to assemble to make a CD to sell at the gigs and help promote his own playing. He spent $1,850 recording the CD at a local recording studio. It cost him an additional $1,000 to have 500 copies of the CD pressed and covers printed. Offering it at gigs and through the mail, Sonny figured that it would take him 2 years to sell all 500 copies of the CD. He did not plan on manufacturing any more copies of the disk, which means that the useful life of the recording is 2 years. Sonny's accountant will divide the recording costs of $1,850 by 24 (months) and write them (amortize) over 2 years. The costs of the disks themselves will be expensed as sold on Sonny's Schedule C as "cost of goods sold" each CD cost

$2 to manufacture, so Sonny will expense $2 on his tax return for each CD he sells (or gives away as promotion). Unsold CDs will become inventory. Sonny may even have to collect state sales tax on a sale, depending on the regulations of the state Sonny is selling in.

A friend of Sonny's recommended that he spend some time out in LA to "see what was going on." Sonny flew out to LA and spent a week hearing music and visiting with some musician buddies he had in California. He had a tax-deductible lunch with a studio owner where he discussed the possibility of getting some studio gigs. He even sat in at some clubs, so he got a chance to play. Unfortunately for Sonny there was little deductible about the trip, he had no income from it and it had no defined, specific business purpose, thus no travel deductions!

At year-end Sonny lucked on to some studio work in New Orleans. He flew to there for four days of studio work and decided to stay on for two extra days to "hang out." Because the primary reason for the trip was business he will be able to write-off the full cost of the flight. He will be able to deduct meals, lodging and incidentals only for the four days he was employed doing the session work. The extra days will be considered vacation. If the ratio between vacation and workdays were reversed Sonny would not be able to write off any of his flight down to New Orleans because the trip would shift from being primarily business to personal.

Sonny thought a personal Website where he could post his resume, pictures, some sound clips from the new CD by The Over the Hill Gang and perhaps some video clips from performances would be great. He also wanted to promote his teaching. The costs of setting up the Website, registering the domain name and hosting the site will all be deductible. The IRS stipulates that Website development be written off (amortized) over 3 years. So all Sonny's costs of designing and setting up the site will be added up (capitalized) and expensed over 3 years.

When Sonny met with his accountant at year-end to do some tax planning and check on his estimated tax payments for the year he had more income than he had expected. His accountant asked if there were some expenses that he could accelerate into the current year; a way he would get the tax benefit of the deductions in the current year. Sonny decided to purchase a new, smaller bass guitar practice amplifier before December 31st. By purchasing the amp before year-end he was able to use the section 179 election and write the new amplifier off 100% in the current year. He can do this even if he charges the amp on his credit card and pays it off in the next year as long as the amp is "in use" before December 31st. Sonny will also have to take a year-end inventory of all the unsold CDs so his accountant can correctly calculate his cost of goods sold.

When he is not on the road Sonny has a room set up in his house that he uses exclusively to give bass guitar lessons. Sonny has about 10 regular students. He uses Form 8829 to take a home office deduction for his music room. He can also deduct the books, instructional videos and supplies that he uses in his teaching.

Internet Resources for Musicians & Singers

The Internet has become a tremendous source of information for musicians and singers – these are some of the Websites I have found useful:

The first, of course, is the official Website of this very book—www.arts-tax-info.com—there you can print and download various checklists and work-sheets, links to the Websites listed below and get updates on all the latest tax changes that affect musicians.

www.billboard-online.com – Billboard Magazine
www.gigmag.com – Gig Magazine
www.recordingmag.com – Music Maker Publications online
www.professional-sound.com – Professional Sound Magazine online
www.livesoundint.com – Live Sound International
www.tourdates.com – Tourdates.com
www.riaa.com – Recording Industry Association of America
www.billboardtalentnet.com – Billboards Talent Net
www.bmi.com – Broadcast Music, Inc.
www.aes.org – Audio Engineering Society
www.afm.org – American Federation of Musicians
www.cmj.com/ – CMJ New Music Report Website
www.americansongwriter.com/ – American Songwriter Magazine
www.csusa.org – Copyright Society of USA
www.songnet.com/nmbd – Music Business Directory
www.afim.org – Association for Independent Music
www.mpa.org – Music Publishers Association
www.songwriters.org – The Songwriters Guild
www.nmpa.org – National Music Publishers Association
www.filmscoremonthly.com – Film Score Monthly
www.filmmusicmag.com – Film Music Magazine
www.ascap.org – American Society of Composers, Authors & Publishers
www.taxresources.com/ – The Internets best single source of tax related links
www.irs.gov – The Internal Revenue Service
www.info.gov – FCIC National Contact Center – Portal to US Government
    information
www.switchboard.com/ – Find people
www.yahoo.com – Huge portal to all sorts of information, get a personal
    e-mail account and directions anywhere in the country
www.refdesk.com/ – The best single source of information on the Internet

www.allmusic.com – The All Music Guide on the Web
www.pollstar.com – The Concert Hotwire – touring info on the Web
www.ubl.com – the Ultimate Band List on the Web
www.lcweb.loc.gov/copyright – The US Government Copyright Office

Musicians & Singers

Continuing Education

Coaching & Lessons Expense	
Dance Training	
Music - Arrangements	
Tapes, CDs, & Recordings	
Training	
Rents - Rehearsal Hall	
Tickets - Performance Audit/Research	
Voice Training	
Other: _____	

Promotional Expenses

Audition Tapes, Videos, CDs & DVDs	
Business Cards	
Film & Processing	
Website Development & Hosting	
Mailing Supplies - Envelopes, etc.	
Photos - Professional	
Resume and Portfolio Expenses	
Other:_____	

Supplies & Expenses

Uniforms & Formal Wear	
Cleaning (uniforms/formal)	
Recording Studio Costs	
Dues - Union & Professional	
Gifts - Business ($25 maximum per person per year)	
Insurance - Equipment	
Interest - Business Loans	
Strings, picks, cords, reeds, etc	
Instrument & Musical Supplies	
Meals - Business (enter 100% of cost)	
Photocopy - Music, etc.	
Postage & Office Supplies	
Sheet Music	
Publications - Trade	
Rents - Office, Storage, etc.	
Rents - Equipment, etc.	
Repairs - Instruments & Equipment	
Secretarial & Bookkeeping	
Commissions - Agent/Manager	
Other: _____	

Auto Travel (in miles)

Audition Travel	
Business Meetings	
Continuing Education	
Job seeking	
Out-of-Town Business Trips	
Purchasing Job Supplies & Materials	
Professional Society Meetings	
Parking Fees & Tolls ($)	
Other: _____	

Travel - Out of Town

Airfare	
Car Rental	
Parking	
Apartment Rent (jobs lasting less than 1 year)	
Taxi, Train, Bus & Subway	
Lodging (do not combine with meals)	
Meals (do not combine with lodging)	
Laundry and Porter	
Bridge & Highway Tolls	
Telephone Calls (including home)	
Other: _____	

Telephone Costs

Cellular Calls	
FAX Transmissions	
On-line Services	
Paging Service	
Pay Phone	
Toll Calls	
Other: _____	

Equipment Purchases

Answering Machine	
Personal Digital Assistants (PDAs)	
Audio Systems & Amplifiers	
Musical Instruments	
Pager and Recorder	
Software	
Speaker Systems	
Computer & Printer	
Tools & other music supplies	
Other: _____	

5

For Visual Artists Only

In this chapter I will look in detail at the activities of our good friend Liz Brushstroke and the kind of income and deductions she had for the year.

First let's walk through some of the expense items for visual artists specifically. I will note in parentheses the type of record keeping the IRS would require:

1. Union dues, professional societies & organizations (invoices & checks)
2. Professional fees for agents, attorneys & accountants (invoices & checks)
3. Artist registries (both printed and on the Internet) (bills, invoice, credit card receipt or check)
4. Master classes, education and seminars (bills, invoice, credit card receipt or check)
5. Personal photographs and resumes – including videos, CDs, CD-ROMs, DVDs and digital image transfers for use on the Internet or your personal Website (bills, invoices, credit card receipt or checks)
6. Slides of artwork – including all photographers fees, developing, slide copies and digital image transfers to CDs (invoices & checks)
7. Costs of printmaking – Having Giclee or other types of printing done (bills, invoices, checks or credit card receipt)
8. Stationery and postage (sales receipts, credit card receipt & checks)
9. Printing of brochures (invoices & checks)
10. Art books – these may need to be allocated between employment income and contract income (sales receipts, credit card receipt & checks)
11. Telephone and cellular phone – actual business calls on your home phone are deductible, but the IRS does not allow the allocation of the base monthly rate. You can deduct only the actual long distance charges. The same rule is true with your cellular phone service. If you get a second phone line strictly for business then it can be considered 100% deductible (bills & checks)

12. Internet service – for research purposes, business e-mail and e-mail while traveling. Be sure to allocate some of the costs for personal use (bills, invoices & credit card receipt)

13. Visiting galleries and museums to view artwork – I often call this expense line item "research;" others refer to it as "auditing." Whatever you call it, make sure to allocate some of this expense to personal use. After all you must sometimes take part in these activities for personal enjoyment, it can't be all business. I quote to clients the old Wall Street saying, "the pigs get fat and the hogs get slaughtered." This is the type of deduction that you must not get piggy with. While the IRS typically hates this deduction, you can easily argue that the visual artist must engage in these viewings for educational reasons and to keep abreast of trends and dynamics within their profession. In an audit you would need to explain what the professional value was (museum admission stubs, business cards from the gallery & diary entries)

14. Gallery rents or memberships - (invoices & checks)

15. Studio rent – Note: you cannot still maintain a home studio if you rent outside space (bills, invoices & checks)

16. Repair of equipment - Computers, presses, sculpting tools & equipment, photography equipment, etc. (bills, invoices & checks)

17. Tax preparation, bookkeeping & accounting fees (bills, invoices & checks)

18. Entry fees into juried show (copy of entry and checks)

19. Advertisement and listing in arts publications (bills, invoices, credit card receipt or checks)

20. Professional magazines (bills, invoices, credit card receipt or checks)

21. Insurance – This can include riders on your home policy that relate directly to your home studio (bills, invoices & checks)

22. Copyright fees (invoices & checks)

23. Equipment purchases – Tools, presses, camera equipment, welders, computers, printers, etc. (bills, invoices, credit card receipt or checks)

24. Framing & displaying Costs – You can only deduct for the costs of artwork you actually sold, other costs related to unsold work become inventory at year-end (bills, invoices, credit card receipt or checks)

25. Supplies – Like the framing costs listed above keep in mind that you can only deduct for the costs of artwork you actually sold, other costs related to unsold work become inventory at year-end (bills, invoices, credit card receipt or checks)

26. Studio supplies and fixtures (bills, invoices, credit card receipt or checks)

Now, let's see what kind of year our artist Liz had.

During the winter she had a one-artist show of her work at the Dublin gallery. She had to arrange for shipping her artwork to Ireland. She planned to go over to Ireland for the show opening, as the artist's presence generally increases sales, and the gallery owner had arranged for her to give a talk on her artwork while she was there. Liz wanted to make sure the trip would be 100% deductible, so she discussed the trip with her accountant in advance. Her trip was going to last eight days; as it was outside the continental US, she learned that any personal and/or vacation time would have to be limited to no more than 25%. Liz realized she would need to arrange some other business activity beyond the gallery exhibit and talk. Using the Internet she checked with some of the schools in Dublin to see if they were offering a class or seminar that she could attend. She signed up for a seminar being given by a famous Irish art historian on the history of Irish art. She also arranged a studio visit with an Irish landscape painter she admired, and she pre-arranged appointments with some gallery owners that owned galleries in Europe, to see what opportunities might be available beyond Ireland. These other business activities helped Liz make the entire trip deductible and still have some time for tourist activity. She could deduct her flight, the shipping of the artwork to Ireland and back, the 50% allowed for meals, all her hotel costs during the business portion of the trip, her auto rental there, laundry, phone calls home, etc. She will also deduct the costs of the artwork sold, including framing costs as a "cost of goods sold" on her Schedule C. Of course the income from the art she sold will be self-employment income on her Schedule C.

In the spring Liz attended an annual conference of a national women's art organization in Phoenix, Arizona. As an officer in the local chapter of this organization, Liz was expected to be there. The trip gave her a chance to network with fellow artists, an opportunity to see new products that art supply dealers displayed, and show her portfolio to some gallery owners. The organization held educational events for the participants every day and an afternoon of gallery tours. Liz was at the conference for the entire three days she was gone. She made sure that she brought home the convention schedule and related literature and noted which events she attended and when. Liz clearly showed a business purpose and she will be able to deduct the entire trip.

A friend of Liz's recommended that she spend some time in New York City to "see what was happening" in the art scene there. Liz flew to the city and spent a week visiting galleries and museums, staying with artist friends she had in New York. She even did some studio visits with other artists. While she may be able to claim some business entertainment expense for lunch with a gallery owner and she perhaps is able to deduct the costs of attending the museums, unfortunately for Liz there will probably be little to deduct on this trip. She had no income from it, and as far as the IRS is concerned it had no well-defined, specific business purpose, thus few deductions!

Liz was invited to be the juror for a local art show. A small art non-profit decided to have its own juried art show in order to attract more artists from around the region. Liz received a small stipend from the organization. Other than some car mileage, she probably didn't have other expenses connected with this activity.

After her opening in Dublin, Liz decided that she wanted to set up a personal Website where she could post her resume, art images, artist statement, etc. If she were going to expand into Europe it would be very helpful to have a Website for gallery owners to be able to visit and see her latest work. The costs of setting up the Website, registering the domain name and hosting the site will all be deductible. She will be able to deduct the costs of having photos taken and transferred to digital images or possibly scanned for use on the site. The IRS stipulates that Website development is written-off (amortized) over 3 years. So all the costs of designing and setting up the site will be added up (capitalized) and expensed over 3 years.

The look of her new Website pleased Liz so much that she decided to have business cards, stationery and a brochure designed and printed to capitalize on and promote it. To let folks know the Website was up and running she did a postcard mailing. All the costs of printing and postage were fully deductible on Liz's Schedule C. Any brochures remaining unsent at year-end may have to be added to her year-end inventory.

Near the end of the year Liz was in a group show at the New York City gallery. As flying was not as time effective as it once had been she decided to drive to NYC where she attended the opening. She spent the following day at the gallery and in the evening had dinner with the gallery owner to discuss possibilities of future shows. The next day she drove back home. Her entire trip will be deductible, including mileage, tolls, parking, hotel and meals (50%), etc. Sales of artwork in NYC are subject to sales tax, but the since the gallery is the entity actually selling Liz's work, they would have the responsibility for handling this tax.

During the year, Liz entered her work into several juried art shows throughout the country. The entry fees, photographer, costs of developing and sending slides and shipping artwork would all be deductible business expenses on her schedule C. To provide evidence of her ongoing effort to market and sell artwork, Liz saves photocopies of all her entries. These could be very important if Liz is hit with a "hobby loss" audit we discussed in Chapter 2.

Liz set up a large room in her home as a studio that she exclusively uses to make art. She takes a home office deduction for the studio on Form 8829. This form allows her to take a portion of all her general home expenses as a deduction against her art income. If she makes alterations to the room specifically for the art production she can take those expenses 100%. This year Liz installed an air venting system to help extract the paint fumes from the studio when she is working. She also upgraded her electrical system. Liz's accountant will depreciate both of these items.

When she met with her accountant at year-end to do some tax planning and check on her estimated tax payments for the year she had more income than she had anticipated. Her accountant asked if there were some expenses that she could accelerate into the current year; a way she would get the tax benefit of the deductions in the current year. Liz needed more places to store artwork and wanted some new flat files, so she purchased the new files before December 31. By purchasing these before year-end she was able to use the Section 179 election and write them off 100% in the current year. She can do this, even if she charges the files on her credit card and pays it off in the next year, as long as the files are "in use" before December 31.

Her accountant also informed her that she would need a year-end inventory list to estimate the value of her completed artwork that was in stock (unsold) on December 31st. For Liz this would include framing costs on unsold art, her preprinted brochures and stationery and art supplies (*not* including her time and labor). During an audit the IRS will want to see a listing of the unsold artwork and its cost. These figures will become ending inventory in Liz's Schedule C form.

Internet Resources for Visual Artists

The Internet has become a tremendous source of information for the visual artist – these are some of the Websites I have found useful:

The first, of course, is the official Website of this very book– www.arts-tax-info.com—there you can print and download various checklists, links to the Websites listed below and get updates on all the latest tax changes that affect visual artists.

www.wwar.com – Worldwide Arts Resources
www.nyfa.org/vaih – New York Foundation for the Arts
www.passion4art.com – Passion4art Website
www.artaccess.com – Art Access Website
www.photoresource.com – Photo Resource Magazine
www.artmarketing.com – ArtNetwork
www.art.net – Art on the Net
www.ilpi.com/artsource – ArtSource Website
www.tfaoi.com/newsmus.htm – Resource Library Magazine listing of art
    museums
www.galleryguide.org – The official Gallery Guide website

www.absolutearts.com – Home of "absolutearts.com"
www.artnewsonline.com/ – ARTnews Magazine
www.artchive.com – The Artchive
www.artsbusiness.com/ – Art Business Exchange
www.artcalendar.com – Art Calendar Magazine – Business Magazine for
    Visual Artists
www.museumgoer.com – The Museums Website
www.sabine-mag.com/ – Sabine Magazine
www.icom.org/vlmp/ – The Virtual Library Museums Page
www.artbytemag.com – Artbyte – The Magazine of Digital Culture
www.photomarketing.com – Photo Marketing Association International
www.photoinsider.com – Photo Insider Magazine
www.gag.org – Graphics Artist Guild
www.theartbiz.com – Website devoted to the business of art
www.taxresources.com/ – The Internets best single source of tax related links
www.irs.gov – The Internal Revenue Service
www.info.gov – FCIC National Contact Center – Portal to US Government
    information
www.switchboard.com/ – Find people
www.yahoo.com – Huge portal to all sorts of information, get a personal
    e-mail account and directions anywhere in the country
www.refdesk.com/ – The single best source of information on the Internet
www.lcweb.loc.gov/copyright – The US Government Copyright Office

Painters, Photographers, & Other Visual Artists

Continuing Education		Auto Travel (In miles)	
Private Lessons		Museum & Gallery Visits	
Master Classes & Apprenticeships		Client & Business Meetings	
Schools & Conferences		Continuing Education	
Tickets to Special Exhibits		Gallery Interviews (Potential Shows)	
Gallery Visits & Talks		Out-Of-Town Business Trips	
Museum Memberships		Purchasing Art Supplies & Materials	
Other: _____		Professional Society Meetings	
Promotional Expenses		Parking Fees & Tolls ($)	
Portfolio Costs		Other: _____	
Business Cards & Resume		**Travel - Out of Town**	
Website Development & Hosting		Airfare & Auto Rental	
Postage & Shipping		Van Rental for Moving of Artwork	
Slide and Photographer Fees		Parking	
Printing of Show Announcement Cards		Taxi, Train, Bus & Subway	
Shows & Exhibits		Lodging (do not combine with meals)	
Printing Costs		Meals (enter 100% of expense)	
Other: _____		Laundry, Maid, & Porter	
Supplies & Expenses		Tolls	
Gallery Memberships and Dues		Telephone Calls (including home)	
Brushes & Cleaning Supplies		Other: _____	
Paints, Film, Papers, etc.		**Telephone Costs**	
Gifts - Business ($25 per person limit)		Paging Service	
Chemicals for Film Processing		Internet and on-line Services	
Museum Dues and Memberships		Pay Phone & Toll Calls	
Canvas and Stretchers		Cellular Phone	
Framing Costs		Other: _____	
Meals - Business (enter 100% of cost)		**Equipment Purchases**	
Slide & Film Processing		Phone & Answering Machine	
Stationary & Office Supplies		Computer, peripherals, & software	
Rent - Studio & Gallery Space		Press, Easel, and Paint Box	
Art Magazines and Books		Darkroom Equipment	
Legal & Accounting Fees		Camera (Digital & Traditional) & Lens	
Rents & Repairs of Equipment		Safety equipment & fixtures	
Sculpture Supplies & Hardware		Kiln & Foundry	
Food & Wine - Gallery Openings		Framing Apparatus	
Modeling Fees & Props		Power & Hand Tools	
Commissions - Agent/Gallery		Sculpting Tools & Equipment	
Other: _____		Other: _____	

6

For Writers Only

In this chapter I will look in detail at the activities of our good friend Guy Focal and the kind of income and deductions he had for the year.

First, let's walk through some of the expense items for writers specifically. I will note in parentheses the type of record keeping the IRS would require:

1. Union dues, professional societies & organizations (invoices & checks)
2. Professional fees for agents, attorneys & accountants (invoices & checks)
3. Classes, education and seminars (bills, credit card receipt & checks)
4. Personal photographs and resumes (bills, credit card receipt & checks)
5. Stationery and Postage (bills, credit card receipt & checks)
6. Books on writing – these may need to be allocated between employment income and contract income (sales receipts, credit card receipt & checks)
7. Telephone and cellular phone – actual business calls on your home phone are deductible, but the IRS does not allow the allocation of the base monthly rate. You can deduct only the actual long distance charges. The same rule is true with your cellular phone service. If you get a second phone line strictly for business then it can be considered 100% deductible (bills & checks)
8. Internet service – for research purposes, business e-mail and e-mail while traveling. Be sure to allocate some of the costs for personal use (bills, checks, invoices & credit card receipt)
9. Purchasing books – be sure to allocate some book purchases to personal use. After all you must sometimes be reading for personal enjoyment, it can't be all business. While the IRS typically hates this deduction you can easily argue that the writer must read competitors' books to keep abreast of trends and dynamics within their profession. In an IRS audit you would need to explain specifically what the professional value was (bills, invoices & checks)

10. Viewing theatre and films (live and via DVD, video and cable) – This is for screen and play writers. I often call this expense line item "research"; others refer to it as "performance audit." Whatever you call it, like the purchase of books listed above make sure to not get "piggy." I often quote to clients the old Wall Street saying, "the pigs get fat and the hogs get slaughtered." As with the previous entry, the IRS dislikes the deduction, but you can easily argue that the stage & screenwriter must engage in these viewings to keep abreast of trends and dynamics within their profession. In an audit you would need to explain specifically what the professional value was (ticket stubs, receipts & diary entries)

11. Office rent – you must be able to prove you need an outside office, you cannot maintain a tax deductible home studio if you rent outside space (bills, invoices & checks)

12. Repair of equipment - Computers, typewriters, etc. (bills, checks, invoices & credit card receipt)

13. Tax preparation, bookkeeping & accounting fees (bills, invoices & checks)

14. Advertisement and listing in publications and on the Internet (bills, checks, invoices & credit card receipt)

15. Professional magazines (bills, checks, invoices & credit card receipt)

16. Insurance – This can include riders on you home policy that relate directly to your home office (bills, invoice & check)

17. Copyright fees (invoice & check)

18. Equipment purchases Computer and office equipment (bills, checks, invoices & credit card receipt)

19. Office supplies and fixtures (bills, checks, invoices & credit card receipt)

Now, let's see what kind of year our writer Guy had.

In the winter, Guy attended an annual conference of a well-known writers organization in New York City. Guy is involved in the local chapter of this organization and represented it at the conference. The trip gave him a chance to network with fellow writers and talk to some of the publishers that were present. The organization sponsors a series of educational events for the participants every day. Guy was at the conference for the entire three days he was gone. He made sure that he brought home the conference schedule and related literature and noted which events he attended. Guy can clearly show a business purpose; he will be able to deduct the entire trip.

Over the summer Guy got a freelance assignment to write a travel article on Texas. Although he was familiar with Texas he decided a visit would help in writing the article and he contacted the Texas Department of Tourism for help. He informed them that he only had a few days in which to travel in the state. They arranged a route that allowed him to hit the high spots in the least amount of time. He incurred the costs of travel, auto rental, meals & hotel, because the magazine that hired him did not directly pick up any of the costs of the trip. The trip had a clearly defined business purpose so the costs were 100% deductible against the income he received from the article.

The president of a national bookstore chain contacted Guy to ask if he would be interested in making some appearances at her stores. She liked Guy's children's books and felt his visit could help in promoting the chain's children's book departments. She wanted Guy to come to her stores in San Francisco, Cleveland, New York and Boston and do a reading and sign books for the children in each one. The owner did not want to get involved in reimbursing expenses, so she offered Guy a straight fee for the appearances from which he would cover all his expenses. All the costs associated with the travel, meals, etc. would be deductible against the income. Like the preceding example the income form this activity would be reported on Guy's Schedule C.

Guy decided that he wanted a personal Website where he could post his resume, excerpts and reviews from his books and articles, etc. He will also use the Website to directly sell copies of his children's books. His illustrator agreed to let him post copies of some of the illustrations she did for his books. The costs of setting up the Website, registering the domain name and hosting the site are all deductible. Guy will be able to deduct the costs of having photos taken and transferred to digital images and of scanning the book illustrations for use on the site. The IRS stipulates that Website development is written-off (amortized) over 3 years. So all the costs of designing and setting up the site will be added up (capitalized) and expensed over 3 years.

In the fall, a well-known TV host asked Guy to appear on a panel on her show to discuss the current state of children's books in America. Guy was to be paid a small stipend and all his costs would be covered directly by the television network. To be on the show Guy flew to California one day and came back the next day, incurring absolutely no tax-deductible expenses on the trip.

In his home Guy has a room set up as an office that he exclusively uses to write in. He uses Form 8829 to take a home office deduction for the office. This form allows him to take a portion of all his general home expenses as a deduction against his freelance writing income. If he makes alterations to the room specifically for the writing he can take those expenses 100%. This year Guy had to upgrade his electrical system to power the office equipment he now has in the office; he also installed a cable modem for Internet access. Guy's accountant will depreciate both of these items. In order to preserve the IRS rules regarding "exclusive use" Guy will have to be very careful about family use of the home office room.

An extensive children's book collection came on the market in the fall;

some of the books were very valuable and collectable, some were not. He called his tax advisor to ask if this purchase would be deductible and the advisor told him that it was not a clear cut deduction, that Guy would have to explain to the IRS how he was actually using the collection in his work as a children's author. Otherwise the IRS would consider the books to be collectors' items and not deductible. If he could justify the deduction, it would be depreciated over 5 years.

One of Guy's children's books was up for an award and he decided to take the trip to LA for the November ceremony with his wife. So, they flew to LA on Friday evening. They wanted to be in time for the related conference being held Saturday. They attended the award ceremony on Saturday evening; the couple spent Sunday in LA and returned home Sunday night. The airline ticket home Sunday would be deductible as it was impractical for the couple to fly home late on Saturday night. All the costs of the trip will be deductible for Guy; none of the costs will be deductible for his wife's travel. He will have to subtract the cost of her airline ticket and adjust for the extra cost of a double room at the hotel. He will also only be able to take the cost of *his* meals.

Over the course of the year Guy kept writing and submitting work to various magazines and publishers throughout the country. His accountant recommended that Guy send all submissions via registered mail with copies attached of the piece and retain all responses from the editors and publishers. These could be very important if Guy is ever hit with a "hobby loss" audit. Of course all the postage, copies, etc would be deductible against Guy's schedule C income.

When Guy met with his accountant at year-end to do some tax planning and check on his estimated tax payments for the year he had more income than he had anticipated. Guy had royalty income from his books as well as income from magazine articles, the book tour and the stipend from his TV appearance. His accountant asked if there were some expenses that he could accelerate into the current year; a way he would get the tax benefit of the deductions in the current year. Guy had been thinking about buying a new computer. He decided to purchase the new computer before December 31. By purchasing before year-end he was able to use the Section 179 election and write it off 100% in the current year. He can do this, even if he charges the computer on his credit card and pays it off in the next year, as long as the computer is "in use" before December 31.

For some work on one of his books Guy had paid one of his illustrators $1,450 during the year. His accountant told him that he needed to issue the illustrator a 1099–MISC, because the amount was in excess of $600. Guy called the illustrator, verified her name, address and got social security number, so that the accountant could prepare the form and mail it to her by the January 31st deadline.

Internet Resources for Writers

The Internet has become a tremendous source of information for the writer – these are some of the Websites I have found useful:

The first, of course, is the official Website of this very book—www.arts -tax-info.com—there you can print and download various checklists, links to the Websites listed below and get updates on all the latest tax changes that affect writers.

www.writerswebsite.com – Great sources and links, particularly for screen-writers
www.nwu.org – National Writers Union
www.publaw.com – Publishing Law Center
www.writerstoolbox.com – The Writers Toolbox
www.poewar.com – The Writer's Resource Center
www.ascap.com – The American Society of Composers, Authors and Pub-lishers
www.wga.org – Writers Guild of America
www.writerswrite.com – The Writers Write Resource
www.bookweb.org – The American Booksellers Association
www.asja.org – The American Society of Journalists and Authors
www.authorsandpublishers.org – The National Association of Authors and Publishers
www.authorsguild.org – The Authors Guild
www.webcom.com/registry – The Authors Registry
www.the-efa.org– The Editorial Freelancers Association
www.gag.org – The Graphics Artist Guild
www.bookwire.com – Home of "bookwire.com"
www.nationalwriters.com – The National Writers Association
www.pen.org – PEN's official Website
www.spawn.org – The Small Publishers, Artists and Writers Network
www.spj.org – The Society of Professional Journalists
www.refdeck.com – The Single Best Source of Facts on the Internet
www.lcweb.loc.gov/copyright – The US Government Copyright Office
www.writersdigest.com – Writers Digest
www.taxresources.com/ – The Internet's best single source of tax related links
www.irs.gov – The Internal Revenue Service
www.info.gov – FCIC National Contact Center – Portal to US Government information
www.switchboard.com/ – Find people
www.yahoo.com – Huge portal to all sorts of information, get a personal e-mail account and directions anywhere in the country

Writers

Professional Fees & Dues		Supplies & Other Expenses	
Association & Union Dues		Briefcase	
Credentials		Business Meals (enter 100% of expenses)	
License		Business Cards	
Professional Associations		Clerical Service	
Union Dues		Computer Software	
Other: _____		Computer Supplies	
Continuing Education		Customer Lists	
Correspondence Course Fees		Entertainment (enter 100% of expense)	
College Courses		Equipment Repair	
Courses Registration		FAX Supplies	
Materials & Supplies		Gifts & Greeting Cards	
Photocopy Expense		On-Line Charges	
Reference Material		Legal & Professional Services	
Books Purchased for Research		Office Expenses	
Seminar Fees		Photocopying	
Textbooks		Postage & Shipping	
Other: _____		DVDs, Films & Videos for Research	
Telephone Expenses		Stationery	
FAX Transmissions		Website Development & Hosting	
Paging Service		Other: _____	
Toll, Cellular, and Pay Calls		*Equipment Purchases*	
Other: _____		Cellular Phone	
Auto Travel (In miles)		FAX Machine, Calculator, and Copier	
Between Jobs or Locations		Pager, Recorder, PDA and Phone	
Client & Publisher Meetings		Computers and Printers	
Continuing Education		Modems and computer peripherals	
Job Seeking		Other:_____	
Out of Town Business Trips		*Travel - Out of Town*	
Purchasing Job Supplies & Materials		Airfare	
Professional Society Meetings		Car Rental, Taxi, Bus, Train, and Subway	
Parking Fees and Tolls ($)		Parking and Tolls	
Other: _____		Lodging & Housing (do not combine with meals)	
Miscellaneous Expenses		Meals (do not combine with lodging)	
Liability Insurance - Business		Porter, Bell Captain, and Laundry	
Subscriptions		Telephone Calls (including home)	
Resume		Other:_____	

7

Setting Up a Business Entity

I think of this as the "should I incorporate?" discussion because that invariably seems to be the opening volley on this topic. The artist will generally have talked to a colleague or family member who has told them *they must incorporate immediately* for whatever purpose, most frequently for the extensive tax benefits offered. So let's look at the choices the artist has for setting up a business entity: Sole-Proprietorship, Partnership, Corporation, Limited Liability Company.

The Sole-Proprietorship

So far in this book I have focused on the sole proprietorship, which is how most artists operate. Until the artist sets up a formal entity, he or she is by default a sole-proprietor. The sole-proprietor simply means one owner (even though a husband-wife team can function as joint proprietors). You will be automatically set up as a sole proprietorship if you do nothing else. The main feature of this form is that it is identified and intertwined with you, which gives it both strengths and weaknesses. If the business makes a profit, it is automatically income for you. If the business incurs a debt, it is your personal debt. If the business gets sued, you will be sued personally as well. It gives you complete flexibility that enables you to instantly shift the direction, policies and focus of your company. But, if there is a problem, any damage can potentially extend into your personal life.

The Partnership

When talking to clients I describe the partnership as a multi-person sole-proprietorship because these two entities are taxed in a very similar manner. The sole-proprietorship files its taxes as part of the owners Form 1040, whereas the partnership files its own separate income tax return (on federal Form 1065) that reports the total income and expenses of the business. The partnership then passes the net, "bottom line" income or losses directly to the personal income tax returns of the partners via the federal Form K-1. This means that the partnership itself almost never pays any income tax directly, but passes the income or loss directly to the partners to be dealt with on their personal returns. You can see why partnerships are often referred to as "flow-through" entities, i.e. the income or loss "flows through" the partnership onto the partner's personal income tax return. The partnership does have the unique and critical tax advantage of "special allocations." Simply put, special allocations allow the partnership to customize the distribution of income and loss by mutual consent through the use of the partnership agreement. For instance, two partners may own the business 50%/50%, but choose to split any losses 75%/25% if that yields a better tax result for them. Partnerships can also, if properly structured, have tax advantages relating to film and sound recording activities.

Although easily formed on a handshake, a partnership is rarely as easy to dissolve. It pays to be very careful when forming a partnership. You will get to know all the good and the bad things about your partner. Bad partnerships can destroy friendships; and most importantly you are completely and personally liable for whatever your partner does (we are speaking here of the common general partnership, the exception to this is the limited partnership in which a limited partner has some liability protection). For instance, in a common general partnership if our musician Sonny Phunky takes a partner and the partner signs him up to play a series of engagements with his band, and then skips town with all the money in the partnership bank account, not only will Sonny be out the money, he will also be liable for playing all the gigs.

Partnerships can certainly work, when there is a clear division of responsibilities and abilities. If you are an actor, a musician, a visual artist, or a writer, but you lack management or promotional skills and your paperwork is usually a shambles, a potential partner who is a good agent, meticulous and detail oriented, but does not have your artistic abilities, may be a natural match.

Partnerships are beneficial when you need to raise more capital. A partner's contribution may help to launch your business venture or project. Because of the sums of money involved, many major films are produced within the limited partnership (and its newest relation, the Limited Liability Company or LLC) form of entity. In this case the partnership is a natural way to raise the money for a specific project like a movie, book or other artistic endeavor and then split the profits from it. When the project is completed the partnership will typically dissolve.

If you do contemplate a partnership have an attorney draw up a clearly defined partnership agreement. The agreement should address issues of operation and specify procedures for termination of one of the partners. What if one of the partners dies? Who will do what jobs within the operation of the partnership? How will decisions be made? What happens if you can't agree? Who will pay for what? Settle all these points in advance, before they have a chance to cause disruption in the business. Nothing kills a business faster than feuding partners.

The Corporation

The third form of business is the corporation. Incorporation gives two main advantages:

1. To raise money you can have people invest in your company.
2. Because a corporation exists legally as a separate entity, it provides a liability shield between you and your personal assets and the business. If the company gets sued, you have some (not iron-clad) protection. Company debts are separate from your personal financial situation.

For tax purposes there are two main types of corporations, the subchapter "C" and the subchapter "S" (the letters refer to subchapters of the tax code). Both are corporations in the legal sense but the taxation of income and losses is handled differently.

The "C" Corporation is your standard. All companies listed on the stock exchange are "C" corporations. These corporations can have unlimited shareholders (investors). If one sells 100,000 shares at $10 each, it has a million dollars in capital to work with. The investors can be individuals, mutual funds, companies, etc. "C" corporations pay income tax directly on their profits, which brings in the disadvantage to the "C" corporation, that of double taxation. For example, if your business earns $100,000 in profit, a corporate tax has to be paid first. Then if you draw a salary (for in a corporation you are in fact an employee), you must declare that salary and pay personal income tax. So, the same money gets taxed twice before you get to spend any of it. Recognizing that this was unfair to the small business, the "S" corporation was formed.

The "S" corporation is a "flow-through" entity, much as a partnership. Unlike the "C" corporation "S" Corporation will not pay income tax directly on its profit. Its net income or loss is simply transferred onto the personal income tax returns of the shareholders via the federal Form K–1 (same as the partnership) and the shareholders will pay the income taxes on their share of the profits of the corporation. Be aware that the "S" corporation does not allow the "special allocations" of the partnership. If two shareholders own the corporation 50%/50%, the profits or losses have to be split 50%/50% too.

The standard "C" corporation files Federal form 1120 annually; the "S" corporation files Federal Form 1120S annually.

The Limited Liability Company

A newer form of business entity is the LLC, or Limited Liability Company. If you are considering setting up your business as a partnership, look long and hard at the LLC, which is generally preferable to the standard partnership. The LLC combines many of the features of a partnership with those of an "S" corporation, without the restrictions that applied to S corporations. It allows the reporting of income or loss directly on the personal income tax returns of the "partners" (or "Members" in the case of an LLC), but provides some of the liability protection of a corporation. The LLC is also a "flow-through" entity that generally files the same federal income tax forms as a partnership, Form 1065, and it does allow for the use of "special allocations" we discussed in the section on partnerships. As with a standard partnership, in most states, you do need two individuals to set up an LLC though some states (including California and New York) do allow the "single-person" LLC, which is taxed as a sole-proprietorship.

When and Which Entity Would the Artist Set Up?

In essence artists have three choices of business entity, the sole-proprietorship, partnership/LLC and corporation. First the artist's decides whether he or she even needs to set up a separate business entity. Having decided, he or she must determine the type of entity to create. Deliberations should involve both an attorney and a tax professional. I would generally advise the artist to never set up a business entity without obtaining separate legal and financial/tax advice. Your attorney will explain the legal benefits of setting up a business entity as well as actually create the entity in the legal sense. Your accountant and tax advisor will clarify what new expenses, responsibilities and functions will be entailed in your new business entity. Commonly, the attorney and tax professional will need to confer on behalf of their client because the legal and financial matters are interrelated.

What occasions considering the establishment of a business entity is that the artist has an issue or problem that cannot be solved any other way. Unless there is a clear need or reason to set up an entity, don't consider it. They are costly to set up and maintain unless they can serve a clear and identifiable purpose. Furthermore they complicate the operation of your business. Accounting and tax filings as well as the associated fees increase. With the help of an attorney and an accountant the artist needs to do a careful cost-benefit analysis, which will help him or her decide whether it is worth setting up the business entity (a cost-benefit analysis is where you weigh the cost incurred vs. the benefit received). It might be that personal liability is the issue for the artist. A cost-benefit analysis may find that insurance is a more effective solution. An artist desiring to bring someone into the business might be better served by simply hiring an employee.

So, what are some of the situations or needs that might finally lead the artist to set up a separate business entity?

- Need for the liability protection provided by a corporation or LLC
- Need for more then one owner in the business
- To isolate some specific business venture or project, like a film, book, or musical
- To separate ownership and control of business operations
- To shift income to other family members, associates or friends to take advantage of those individual's lower income tax rates
- To raise capital for a specific venture or project by bringing in investors
- IRS audit concerns, for many years sole-proprietorships have been and probably will continue to be #1 on the IRS audit hit list other formal business entities are less likely to be audit targets
- Tax savings available in particular entities, such as potential payroll tax savings available in "S" corporations
- Working in a multi-state environment – corporations are probably the most portable and practical entity for artists working across state lines

Taking our four artists, let's look at when and why an artist might chose to set up a separate business entity.

Example One

Actor Ima Starr is beginning to hit it big and make some serious money. She decides to set up a corporation for her acting business (sometimes referred to as "loan-out" corporations). With this setup the film companies would pay her corporation for her services and she would in turn be an employee of her own corporation. The benefits to Ima could be that (1) she is able to shift income to later tax years and allow her to delay payment of income taxes, (2) she might save payroll taxes (FICA taxes) by operating as an "S" corporation, (3) she may use the corporation to shift income to other members of her family or household (and into lower tax brackets). The corporation would help her limit her personal liability, and at the same time lower her chances statistically of being audited and it would isolate her business activity from the rest of her life. The IRS frequently zeros in on "loan out" corporations so they have to be structured with great care to sidestep the punitive personal holding company rules.

Ima is also considering an LLC to produce her own film, book or other project. The project would be produced inside the LLC when the project was sold the LLC would distribute the profits to the investors/members and perhaps dissolve. If Ima already has the corporation why would she set up a separate LLC for her film project? She would do this to isolate this one project from the rest of her business activities. From both a legal and financial point of view she would want to do this in order to not involve the individuals that are members of the LLC in her primary operations inside her corporation.

Example Two

Musician Sonny Phunky needs some investor money in order to make a new recording with an orchestra. He could set up an LLC, much the way Ima did, to attract investors and isolate that activity, and later to channel the profits directly to the investors from the ultimate profits of the recording.

Sonny's band, "The Over the Hill Gang" has been discovered and a showcase tour is being planned and Sonny is worried about touring liabilities concerning his band and crew. His lawyer advises him to set up a corporation for the band. Income from the tour will be paid into the corporation and Sonny, the crew and band members will all become employees of the corporation for the tour's duration. This will help limit Sonny's personal liability in case of accidents and other unforeseen problems. Sonny's tax advisor concurred with the lawyer that since the tour was going to take the band to throughout the world, including the U.S. a corporation would probably be the most practical type of entity. His tax advisor also discussed setting up a music equipment leasing company that would own all the equipment used by the band on the tour. Sonny's corporation would then lease (pay rent) to the leasing company for the use of the sound and lighting equipment. If the leasing company was an LLC it would give Sonny an additional layer of liability protection. The leasing company can be set up by Sonny and his attorney using a generic name. A generic name gives Sonny some privacy, in that people need not know that Sonny owns the leasing company. Such a move can be very tax efficient as it gives Sonny another means of receiving profits from the band's activities.

Should Sonny's songwriting continue to grow, as it seems to be now he is considering setting up a second LLC (or other business entity) to control his songwriting activities.

Example Three

Suppose our painter, Liz Brushstroke befriends an individual who becomes her business manager and agent, and as such is a vital and essential part of her artistic activities. Liz decides to make this person a legal part of her business by setting up a corporation or LLC (either one would probably work) and giving him or her a real equity stake in her artistic life. By making this individual a shareholder or member of her business Liz legally recognizes this person's importance in her business life and will be able, depending on how the entity is structured, to give him or her a share of the profits. Liz's advisors told her that she could simply hire her friend as an employee but Liz preferred setting up the business entity.

Liz has an investor interested in funding the publication of a limited edition book of her works, and for this her attorney and tax advisor both recommended an LLC. The LLC will be structured to receive cash from the investor. In turn, it will receive all the income for book sales, pay all the expenses of the publication, then distribute the net profits to Liz and the investor according to their LLC agreement. After all the books are sold, the final profits will be distributed, the LLC would file a final income tax return and fold.

Example Four

Guy Focal has his first big year as a writer when one of his books is sold for a major film adaptation. He decides to incorporate his writing activities and sets up an "S" corporation. His agent or publisher will pay his royalties directly into the corporation from now on. The corporation will allow him to put some family members who are helping him with his correspondence and research on his payroll, thus diversifying his income into their lower tax brackets. The corporation will also give Guy some liability protection.

With knowledge gained from this recent film experience, Guy decides to try and adapt and make a film of another of his books. He finds some investors and sets up an LLC to act as a production company for the film project, because he does not want the investors to be a part of his "S" corporation. If the project doesn't succeed the LLC investors/members will most likely be able to use the losses on their personal income tax returns. If it succeeds and sells the income from the film will become income on the member's income taxes.

In Closing

Some readers may wonder why I put this chapter nearer the end of the book. It may appear to them that this is the first matter we should discuss. Yet, at the beginning of their career very few artists would have any need to set up a formal business structure. Even many successful artists never set up any formal business entity. At the early stage of an artist's career it would rarely be cost effective, and more importantly the direction and scope of the artist's ultimate activity would be insufficiently developed to make effective decisions regarding business structures.

By the way, most of what we have talked about in the book on rules relating to income and expenses still applies to any structure you may happen to operate in. While the mechanics may change, in general, the IRS view of taxable income and what it considers a justifiable expense does not alter much across the spectrum of different business entities.

Please keep in mind that we have barely scratched the surface on this very complex topic. You can see this whole subject is a balancing act between financial, legal, estate and income tax concerns. Any decisions are subjective and relate directly to personal financial goals, so what works for the colleague you spoke to at a party may not work at all for you. Be VERY careful of anything that sounds like a boilerplate solution. I feel that most financial decisions are far more personal then most people realize, and business structure is very much in that camp. Make any decisions in this area after careful discussions of your personal desires, goals and concerns, which would include other strategic issues such as estate planning.

8

The Audit Process, Recordkeeping and Your Taxpayer Rights

An important fact to have firmly in mind as you approach your record keeping and documentation is that IRS audits occur generally 12 to 18 months *after* the end of the tax year being audited. You can very easily be in the position of having as IRS agent ask you detailed questions on a business meal, travel expense or other deduction that happened over two years ago!

Simple mistakes can cause a return to be questioned. These mistakes and oversights can include:

✓ Mathematical errors – Simple, you didn't add or subtract correctly!
✓ Income that was independently reported to the IRS and that its computers couldn't find on your tax return - These can be 1099s and W–2s that the IRS computer scans and cannot match on your return. Sometimes the IRS is correct sometimes it is not.
✓ Social security number and name do not match - In the past several years the IRS has been matching the first 3 characters of all the names against the individual's social security number using the Social Security Administration database. When there isn't a match between the name and social security number you are sent a letter.

How is a return typically selected for audit? The IRS subjects all personal income tax returns to a computerized analysis based on a mathematical technique known as Discriminate Function (DIF), which identifies income tax returns with a high probability of error and a chance of significant tax change. The DIF program evolved from a concern during the 1960s that too many "no change" audits were occurring, and that IRS audits should focus on returns likely to have errors. Under the DIF procedure, returns with high DIF scores or other special features are manually inspected to select some for audit. Thus, the DIF score acts as a red flag for IRS audits. The DIF formula is secret, known to only a very few senior IRS officials. Experience indicates that certain factors are likely to increase the DIF score and the possibility of an audit. Among these factors are high salaries or other compensation, high expenses relative to income, and the presence of certain types of deductions such as charitable contributions and medical expenses. DIF formula data is developed from a range of sources, including IRS audit experience. Unfortunately for many of the readers of this book, self-employed individuals are usually at the top of the IRS's "most audited" list.

Your business code can also subject you to audit. If you are self-employed you will notice that there is a box for an industry code on your Schedule C (box B at the top of the form). This code identifies to the IRS the type of business you are in. Some IRS auditing is being done centering around this code rather than on the actual numbers on the return. In other words, the IRS in your district may be looking into "independent artists, writers & performers" code 711510, and your return could get chosen for a full-blown audit, regardless of your DIF score.

The DIF score is just the first stage of the potential audit process. Once the return is flagged, an IRS examiner will review it to see if he or she thinks it is worth auditing. This same IRS agent is generally the one who decides if your return will actually be audited. If the amounts "flagged" on your return just concern one or two line items, it may be subjected to a "desk audit," which causes you to get a letter asking for substantiation or detail on a particular line item on the return. This type of audit is all done via mail. The taxpayer sends in the supporting documentation, the agent reviews it, and if there are no further questions, the agent lets you know the result.

The second type of audit is of the live and in-person kind. Usually the IRS will ask you to come into their office bringing all your supporting documentation. In some instances, if the audit is big enough, they may choose to visit your place of business. The audit notification will tell you in advance exactly what type of documentation is wanted and what line items on the return are being examined. The IRS does not allow the auditor to turn the audit into a fishing expedition.

The audit can be conducted with the taxpayer or with an authorized representative such as a CPA, Attorney or Enrolled Agent. The taxpayer may bring a professional with him or her.

Audits are usually straightforward affairs, starting with a detailed interview. The interview helps to develop a profile of you, your business and the manner in which you operate your business. You will also be asked questions about your finances as they relate to your tax return.

The audit process is fairly simple: The auditor points to a line on the tax return and asks for all the substantiating documents for that number. For instance, if you are self-employed the agent might ask you for copies of all your bank statements. The agent will add up all your bank deposits for the year and compare them to your total gross income on your Schedule C form. If your

Schedule C form says that your gross income was $50,000 and you, in fact, deposited $75,000 in your bank accounts during the year you'd better be ready to do some explaining! Substantiation for expenses and deductions usually means actual receipts; the IRS does not as a rule accept canceled checks or credit card statements as receipts (though many auditors will in practice, especially when the taxpayer has noted the specifics of the expense on the memo section of the check or on the credit card receipt).

Let's take some examples of the more contentious and difficult areas and see how they might play out during an audit:

1. **Meals & Entertainment expense** – while we know that meals & entertainment are only 50% deductible, they are still a real audit target for the IRS. First the agent will want to see a list of all the meals for the year by amount. This list must equal the total amount of meals that has been put on the tax return. If the list is voluminous you may be asked of the "who, what & where" detail for just a few. You should bring your schedule book/diary with your notations for each meal to the audit so when the agent wants substantiation you can show him or her your entry and explain the reason for the deduction. If the situation was a travel related and you used the government per diem rates, the agent will ask you about the trip itself. If the trip is deductible, the meals are as well. The agent might ask to look at contracts for specific jobs to make sure that the producer or employer was not reimbursing for your meals expense.

2. **Travel** – the agent will want to know what the business purpose was. The less defined and flabbier your argument is, the more likely the agent is to disallow the deduction. Some play-acting on this one might help. You may remember that actor Ima Starr and musician Sonny Phunky both did business trips to LA. Ima did her homework in advance and set up appointments, attended some auditions, and kept a good schedule and diary of events. Sonny just showed up in LA hung out, talked to some folks, then came home. Against the advice of his accountant Sonny decided to deduct the full trip. His interview with the agent might go like this:

Agent: *Sonny, what about this trip to LA?*
Sonny: *Yea, there is a great music scene out there and I wanted to check it out.*
Agent: *Can I see your schedule of the trip; did you plan the trip in advance?*
Sonny: *Well, I didn't have anything scheduled in advance. I just made some calls when I got there.*
Agent: *Did you have business activity everyday?*
Sonny: *Most days I did something, like I had lunch with Sam Smith;*

*he owns a recording studio out there and I talked to him
about getting studio work.*

Agent: *Do you have any evidence of this meeting, did you save his
business card?*

Sonny: *I'm not sure if I still have it.*

And Ima's interview might go this way:

Agent: *Ima, what about this trip to LA?*

  Ima: *I had recently worked on a film with Mel Fun and I made
some connections in LA that I wanted to explore further.*

Agent: *Can I see your schedule of the trip?*

  Ima: *Yes, I have outlined it on this calendar. Most of my appointments and lunch engagements were made in advance. I have
business cards, copies of thank you letters I wrote to the
participants and copies of their replies, if I received any.*

Agent: *Did you have business activity everyday?*

  Ima: *Yes, I had a meeting and/or audition every day. I also spent
some of the time in LA making phone calls, which I have
recorded in my schedule as well.*

Agent: *Did you do anything after you called to follow up?*

  Ima: *I had brought along some videos, my resume and a copy of
my CD. These all had my website listed on them. If the
phone call was positive, I dropped off my package right
away and called back the next day to see if I could get an
appointment before I left LA.*

I think it is clear which trip the agent is likely to allow! Ima did her
homework and focused on the trip in such a way that it would be difficult for the agent to disallow the deduction of her trip.

3. **Mileage** – The agent will want to see a listing of total
mileage for business use for the year, which includes a line
item for each trip, an estimate of miles driven, and a note
what the business purpose was. Though the I.RS likes
odometer readings it does not require them. It is my experience that a reasonable round trip estimate will usually suf-
fice. It is the business purpose that is most important. Most
items on your list will probably be straightforward, such as
trips to your agent's office or to a gig or performance, but the
agent might select a few to ask you about specifically. Obviously, the more business miles you write off the more likely
the agent will question trips.

4. **Research & Performance Audit** – Much of what the IRS is
looking for when its audits the artist is the personal expense

masquerading as business deductions. The agent will questions such things as:

✓ Writers buying books
✓ Actors & other show biz folks buying cable TV service & tickets to movies, plays and shows
✓ Musicians purchasing CDs and tickets to concerts
✓ Visual artists going to museums and galleries

If the agent has an issue with these allowable expenses, he or she might ask for a logbook or diary entry where you listed the exact business purpose of the particular item. A good example of deductible "research" might be when Ima Starr rented Mel Fun's movies in anticipation of performing in his movie, or when Sonny Phunky purchased some CDs to learn songs for his gig with the Butterball Kings. Similarly, our writer Guy purchasing children's books that allow him to monitor his competition and Liz Brushstroke visiting galleries for the same reason.

Unfortunately, what tends to happen in real life is that people simply take a percentage of these costs as "business." Such as the actor sitting with his or her accountant and saying something like, "My total cable bill was $545 and I'd say 40% was business." For an audit you may be able to prove something close to the chosen number, or the agent may feel that the amount appears reasonable and not even question it. The agent may in fact be thrilled that you did not get piggy and try to take the whole $545! But, beware the agent can get real specific on these deductions and make your life miserable.

MSSP – The IRS Audit Training Manuals

It surprises many folks to learn that the IRS actually publishes its training manuals concerning audits, part of its "Market Segment Specialization Program." These manuals can be downloaded from the IRS Website www.irs.gov/prod/bus_info/mssp, and are absolutely indispensable guides. Many industries are covered by the manuals but only three directly concern us.

1. Entertainment Industry

We learn that the IRS is fully cognizant that reimbursements are a common part of the industry. The guide talks at length about SAG, DGA and Equity and tells the agent how reimbursements are handled and what types of things are reimbursed. It instructs the agent to review all employment contracts, including those for product endorsements, to look for reimbursements and "perks" such as free products.

Another interesting audit target is the issue of the "tax home." In recent audits the IRS has been attempting to declare some folks in the entertainment industry "itinerant." If the IRS can declare you an itinerant, then all your travel and meals expenses are blown off the return. After all how can someone with no home deduct expenses for travel while away from home! IRS publication 463 explains the concept of tax home like this:

> *If you do not have a regular or main place of business or work, use the following three factors to see if you have a tax home.*
>
> *1) You perform part of your business in the area of your main home and use that home for lodging while doing business in the area.*
>
> *2) You have living expenses at your main home that you duplicate because your business requires you to be away from that home.*
>
> *3) You have not abandoned the area in which both your traditional place of lodging and your main home are located; you have a member or members of your family living at your main home; or you often use that home for lodging.*
>
> *If you satisfy all three factors, your tax home is the home where you regularly live, and you may be able to deduct travel expenses. If you satisfy only two factors, you may have a tax home depending on all the facts and circumstances. If you satisfy only one factor, you are a transient; your tax home is wherever you work and you cannot deduct travel expenses.*

The tax home issue can sneak up on you in an audit. While you are busy lining up your substantiation and getting worksheets for your expenses, the agent may be deciding to go for a bigger issue and eliminate the travel expense outright!

Because gift giving is so prevalent in the industry, the guide reminds the agent that business gifts are limited to $25 per person per year. On top of that you will still need a receipt and a diary entry describing the "why" of the gift.

Other deductions that the IRS is specifically targeting in its audit guide:

- ✓ Hairstyles
- ✓ Clothing and wardrobe, unless "period" clothing
- ✓ Laundry expense, unless used for deductible clothing
- ✓ Security, bodyguards, and limousines, except when needed for protection at public appearances
- ✓ Make-up, unless stage makeup unsuitable for any other use
- ✓ Physical Fitness, except for the duration of employment requiring

> physical conditioning or if the actors' roles require the mainte-
> nance of body building and/or weight lifting skills
> ✓ Payments to business managers to the extent that the manager is
> engaged in personal bills & affairs
> ✓ Legal expenses if the claim is personal
> ✓ A coach, personal trainer or personal guru
> ✓ Toupees, false teeth, hearing aids, etc.
> ✓ Cosmetic surgery

2. Music Industry

This guide covers songwriters, publishers, managers, producers, music video production and musicians. The music industry guide has two of my favorite quotes in all IRS literature:

1. *The performing artist is usually a very creative person as far as talent goes, but may lack knowledge in understanding bookkeeping, taxes and cash flow.*

2. *Musicians who have not reached an income level sufficient to hire business managers often have a poor record keeping system. This doesn't appear to be due to an intent to cheat or defraud the government; rather, it seems to be due to the taxpayer's basic lack of concern for these types of matters. These taxpayers are artists and are totally committed to their work and doing whatever it takes to become a success. Preparation of their yearly tax returns is an afterthought and the quality of the records they maintain to support their tax return often bears this out.*

The manual is interesting in that it advises the agent not to get too carried away auditing musicians, because the agent can spend a great deal of time fixing "messy" books and then not come up with a deficiency (i.e., CASH!).

The music industry guide is concerned with many of the same items that we see in the entertainment guide, such as personal items being deducted as business expenses. The guide discusses the musical entertainer's argument that they must maintain a "look" for the benefit of their fans, and that it will be on this basis that the musician attempts to deduct a variety of clothing and other personal items. The guide warns that "while the taxpayer's argument is not totally without merit and can even sound reasonable," the agent should not allow the performer to deduct personal expenses.

A key focus for the auditor appears to be unreported income. The guide mentions that while royalties will be reported (Form 1099–MISC), the musician might well have freelance income from performing that will go unreported. The guide also acknowledges the prevalence of trades and trading in the music industry. The IRS considers trades are income too.

The guide tells the agent to review contracts to see if expenses were re-imbursed. If the agent is auditing a "star" who paid all the expenses of the band and crew while on the road, it instructs the agent to selectively sample some returns from these folks, to see if they had double dipped and taken travel expenses. The agent is informed that it may be necessary to cross check "related returns of taxpayers in the music industry due to the close working relationships between taxpayers in the industry."

3. Artist & Art Galleries

With this guide the IRS is mainly concerned with actual galleries and gallery owners more than with visual artists, but it does contain some items of inter-est. It tells the agent to be aware of the prevalence of trading between artists and gallery owners. The agent is told that the trades are often not even re-ported in the books of the gallery. Should the IRS audit a gallery that has un-reported income from trades with artists, you can be sure that the next thing it is going to do is look at the artist's return to see whether the trade was re-ported there. In general, the guide warns the auditor to look out for unreported income. It mentions inventory as being an error prone item on the artist's re-turn. The error arises because the visual artist does not correctly account for framing and supplies that are left unsold at year-end.

Audit Etiquette

Most IRS agents who I have dealt with are fair and reasonable people. This is not to say that you will not have arguments and subsequent appeals but many issues can be settled on the agent's level. Characteristically IRS agents are classic bureaucrats: they want to process your audit and get it off their desks as soon as possible. Usually that's how the taxpayer feels about the audit as well! Here are some pointers:

1. Be fully prepared with details on only the item the agent requested, and no more. Do not bring anything extra to the audit. Answer ques-tions as simply and with as little embellishment as possible.

    In the long run you will benefit if you give detailed and complete information and are forthcoming in your answers. Approaching the audit this way will often keep the agent from delving deeper into the return. I liken IRS agents to thieves looking for a car with the keys still in the ignition. If you give the agent the feeling right off the bat that you have your act together and are fully prepared, it can have the effect of taking the agent off his or her guard.

    For instance, if one of the audit items is car mileage and you pro-vide a neatly typed list outlining each trip, the miles driven, and the business purpose, the agent might not ask any specific questions, but simply take a copy of the list for his or her files. You would follow the same procedure for all the questioned items: have a list of each deduction, including amounts and description, to give the agent. Receipts should accompany each list. From a voluminous list, the agent might just pick a few receipts to audit.

2. An old canard suggests bringing in messy receipts and "letting them do the work." I don't agree with that. You should appear as neat and be as forthcoming as possible. Incidents have been reported of the agent being given less than complete records and receipts, but because the package was so neat and orderly, he or she assumed it was complete and didn't even review the package!

3. Never cop an attitude or try to "snow" the agent in any way! I know quite a few IRS agents and, believe me, they have seen and heard it all. Treat the experience as a task (however unpleasant) that has to be worked through. Treat the agent with respect and courtesy and make sure your tax professional does the same. Try to settle matters on the agent level. If you ultimately need to fight something, that's OK, just don't make it a first impulse.

4. NEVER go to any audit without a tax professional. As a tax professional I prefer to have the taxpayer present as I feel the taxpayer is usually the best one to answer the larger questions relating to their business. A lot of responses to auditor questions do rely on some judicial "spin-doctoring" though. More play acting is in order here:

> **Agent:** *Ima, what about this meal with Joe Blow on October 15?*
>   **Ima:** *Joe is casting a new film that has a part for a sultry lounge singer that I would be perfect for.*
> **Agent:** *So what did you do to try to get the part?*
>   **Ima:** *I didn't want to directly discuss business during the lunch. I was just trying to get to know him a little and butter him up a bit. Right after the lunch I sent him a nice letter and copies of my resume, CD and a video of my singing with The Blue Jazzbos so he would know that I could sing as well as act.*
> **Agent:** *So what happened?*
>   **Ima:** *Unfortunately I did not get the part.*

This is how she should have responded:

> **Agent:** *Ima, what about this meal with Joe Blow on October 15?*
>   **Ima:** *Joe is casting a new film that has a part for a sultry lounge singer that I would be perfect for.*
> **Agent:** *So what did you do to try to get the part?*

> **Ima:** *While we had lunch, I pitched him the idea of doing the part and gave him copies of my resume, CD and a video of my singing with The Blue Jazzbos so he would know that I could sing as well as act.*
>
> **Agent:** *So what happened?*
>
> **Ima:** *Unfortunately I didn't get the part.*

Don't forget, there has to be business transacted at some point during the meal or the IRS is going to disallow it. Whether Ima got the part does not matter; the deduction will stand or fall on its own merits. It doesn't really matter if there is a specific part she is going after, she can be taking Joe out to let him know she is available for consideration for any parts he may have.

Is it possible for an actor to be allowed a deduction for over the counter makeup or the musician to be allowed a write off for a business lunch where no business was transacted? Definitely yes! Could the visual artist get audited and not be questioned about ending inventory or the writer not have the IRS agent even ask about his travel deduction? Yes again! There is always a chance that the agent will not ask about a particular deduction. You might have an inexperienced agent who accepts your justification for a deduction as valid. Conversely, you may have an agent unfamiliar with your business as an artist who makes you justify and argue everything.

I don't necessarily try to "make friends" with the agent. At its core it is an adversarial relationship. A measure of cordial respectfulness is best.

Develop a strategy with your tax professional before you even meet with the agent and assess your weaknesses and strengths. By going to an audit with a strategy the process is less likely that will get out of control. Your tax professional may see from the outset the course the audit might follow. A writer with 5 years of continuous losses would want to be ready to deal with the "hobby loss" matter. A visual artist that had never listed an ending inventory would want to be ready to answer questions on that. A musician or film director with high travel and meals would want to be ready to address those questions.

Recordkeeping

We have discussed record keeping throughout the book without addressing how to actually do it. Our Website www.arts-taxinfo.com has some very handy Microsoft® Excel® downloadable worksheets for simple organization of income and expenses. There are also many great computer programs for this purpose and I can recommend three that I like, and list the Websites where you can get some additional information on each one:

1. Quicken®– www.quicken.com
2. Microsoft® Money® – www.msmoney.com
3. QuickBooks® – www.quickbooks.com (for those needing more advanced accounting features)

Once these programs are set up properly, they do a great job and are easy to operate; they will be an enormous help at year-end. Purchase an accordion file at an office supply store to keep your receipts in. If you'd rather not work on the computer, you can use the handy worksheets at the back of this book. I also have these sheets available on the Website www.arts-taxinfo.com as printable forms and Microsoft® Excel® downloadable worksheets.

Consider hiring a good bookkeeper if you are too busy in your professional life to do the record keeping. Bookkeeping help is relatively inexpensive and can save you a world of headaches.

Your Rights as a Taxpayer

Several years ago the IRS created a publication that explains your rights as a taxpayer. It includes an eight-part "Declaration of Taxpayer Rights," as well as a section on audits, appeals, collections and refunds. Here is the text of Publication 1:

DECLARATION OF TAXPAYER RIGHTS

I. PROTECTION OF YOUR RIGHTS

IRS employees will explain and protect your rights as a taxpayer throughout your contact with us.

II. PRIVACY AND CONFIDENTIALITY

The IRS will not disclose to anyone the information you give us, except as authorized by law. You have the right to know why we are asking you for information, how we will use it, and what happens if you do not provide requested information.

III. PROFESSIONAL AND COURTEOUS SERVICE

If you believe that an IRS employee has not treated you in a profes-sional, fair, and courteous manner, you should tell that employee's supervisor. If the supervisor's response is not satisfactory, you should write to the IRS director for your area or the center where you file your return.

IV. REPRESENTATION

You may either represent yourself or, with proper written authoriza-tion, have someone else represent you in your place. Your represen-tative must be a person allowed to practice before the IRS, such as an attorney, certified public accountant, or enrolled agent. If you are in an interview and ask to consult such a person, then we must stop and reschedule the interview in most cases.

You can have someone accompany you at an interview. You may make sound recordings of any meetings with our examination, appeal, or collection personnel, provided you tell us in writing 10 days before the meeting.

V. PAYMENT OF ONLY THE CORRECT AMOUNT OF TAX

You are responsible for paying only the correct amount of tax due under the law—no more, no less. If you cannot pay all of your tax when it is due, you may be able to make monthly installment payments.

VI. HELP WITH UNRESOLVED TAX PROBLEMS

The Taxpayer Advocate Service can help you if you have tried unsuccessfully to resolve a problem with the IRS. Your local Taxpayer Advocate can offer you special help if you have a significant hardship as a result of a tax problem. For more information, call toll free 1-877-777-4778 (1-800-829-4059 for TTY/TDD) or write to the Taxpayer Advocate at the IRS office that last contacted you.

VII. APPEALS AND JUDICIAL REVIEW

If you disagree with us about the amount of your tax liability or certain collection actions, you have the right to ask the Appeals Office to review your case. You may ask a court to review your case.

VIII. RELIEF FROM CERTAIN PENALTIES AND INTEREST

The IRS will waive penalties when allowed by law if you can show you acted reasonably and in good faith or relied on the incorrect advice of an IRS employee. We will waive interest that is the result of certain errors or delays caused by an IRS employee.

EXAMINATIONS, APPEALS, COLLECTIONS, AND REFUNDS

EXAMINATIONS (AUDITS)

We accept most taxpayers' returns as valid. If we inquire about your return or select it for examination, it does not suggest that you are dishonest. The inquiry or examination may or may not result in more tax. We may close your case without change; or, you may receive a refund.

The process of selecting a return for examination usually begins in one of two ways. First, we use computer programs to identify re-

turns that may have incorrect amounts. These programs may be based on information returns, such as Forms 1099 and W–2, on studies of past examinations, or on certain issues identified by compliance projects. Second, we use information from outside sources that indicates that a return may have incorrect amounts. These sources may include newspapers, public records, and individuals. If we determine that the information is accurate and reliable, we may use it to select a return for examination.

Publication 556, Examination of Returns, Appeal Rights, and Claims for Refund, explains the rules and procedures that we follow in examinations. The following sections give an overview of how we conduct examinations.

By Mail

We handle many examinations and inquiries by mail. We will send you a letter with either a request for more information or a reason why we believe a change to your return may be needed. You can respond by mail or you can request a personal interview with an examiner. If you mail us the requested information or provide an explanation, we may or may not agree with you, and we will explain the reasons for any changes. Please do not hesitate to write to us about anything you do not understand.

By Interview

If we notify you that we will conduct your examination through a personal interview, or you request such an interview, you have the right to ask that the examination take place at a reasonable time and place that is convenient for both you and the IRS. If our examiner proposes any changes to your return, he or she will explain the reasons for the changes. If you do not agree with these changes, you can meet with the examiner's supervisor.

Repeat Examinations

If we examined your return for the same items in either of the 2 previous years and proposed no change to your tax liability, please contact us as soon as possible so we can see if we should discontinue the examination.

APPEALS

If you do not agree with the examiner's proposed changes, you can appeal them to the Appeals Office of IRS. Most differences can be settled without expensive and time-consuming court trials. Your appeal rights are explained in detail in both Publication 5. Your

Appeal Rights and How To Prepare a Protest If You Don't Agree, and Publication 556, Examination of Returns, Appeal Rights, and Claims for Refund.

If you do not wish to use the Appeals Office or disagree with its findings, you may be able to take your case to the U.S. Tax Court, U.S. Court of Federal Claims, or the U.S. District Court where you live. If you take your case to court, the IRS will have the burden of proving certain facts if you kept adequate records to show your tax liability, cooperated with the IRS, and meet certain other conditions. If the court agrees with you on most issues in your case and finds that our position was largely unjustified, you may be able to recover some of your administrative and litigation costs. You will not be eligible to recover these costs unless you tried to resolve your case administratively; including going through the appeals system, and you gave us the information necessary to resolve the case.

COLLECTIONS

Publication 594, The IRS Collection Process, explains your rights and responsibilities regarding payment of federal taxes. It describes:

- *What to do when you owe taxes. It describes what to do if you get a tax bill and what to do if you think your bill is wrong. It also covers making installment payments, delaying collection action, and submitting an offer in compromise.*
- *IRS collection actions. It covers liens, releasing a lien, levies, releasing a levy, seizures and sales, and release of property.*

Your collection appeal rights are explained in detail in Publication 1660, Collection Appeal Rights.

Innocent Spouse Relief

Generally, both you and your spouse are responsible, jointly and individually, for paying the full amount of any tax, interest, or penalties due on your joint return. However, if you qualify for innocent spouse relief, you may not have to pay the tax, interest, and penalties related to your spouse (or former spouse). For information on innocent spouse relief and two other ways to get relief, see Publication 971, Innocent Spouse Relief, and Form 8857, Request for Innocent Spouse Relief (And Separation of Liability and Equitable Relief).

REFUNDS

You may file a claim for refund if you think you paid too much tax. You must generally file the claim within 3 years from the date you filed your original return or 2 years from the date you paid the tax, whichever is later. The law generally provides for interest on your refund if it is not paid within 45 days of the date you filed your return or claim for refund. Publication 556, Examination of Returns, Appeal Rights, and Claims for Refund, has more information on refunds.

If you were due a refund but you did not file a return, you must file within 3 years from the date the return was originally due to get that refund.

9

Choosing a Tax Advisor

There are two main characteristics you look for in a tax professional. I call them the two "*Cs*":

1. Competence and
2. Communication.

The accountant/client relationship is a symbiotic association, where the accountant has the knowledge, and is able to communicate the information that the client needs to take full advantage of that knowledge.

There are two main designations for tax professionals that might affect your choice of one.

The first is the C.P.A. (Certified Public Accountant). The CPA is an individual who has successfully completed the Uniform CPA Examination. This exam is given over a two-day period twice annually (in May and November), and consists of four sections: Business Law & Professional Responsibilities; Auditing; Accounting & Reporting-Taxation, Managerial, and Governmental and Not-for-Profit Organizations; and Financial Accounting & Reporting-Business Enterprises. The exam is not principally concerned with taxation; therefore the CPA designation, while important, does not necessarily guarantee competence in tax matters. The CPA is required to meet stringent standards of state licensing, ethics and educational requirements, and this should give the client some comfort that the CPA is honest and professional.

The second designation is that of the E.A. (Enrolled Agent), and is bestowed directly by the Internal Revenue Service. They explain it this way:

> *An enrolled agent is a person who has earned the privilege of practicing, that is, representing taxpayers, before the Internal Revenue Service. Enrolled agents, like attorneys and certified public accountants (CPAs), are generally unrestricted as to which taxpayers they can represent, what types of tax matters they can handle, and which IRS offices they can practice before. In contrast, practice before the IRS is much more limited for other individuals such as unenrolled tax*

*return preparers, family members, full time employees, partners, and
corporate officers.*

To become an Enrolled Agent the individual must take a grueling two-day
test that centers on taxation. The Enrolled Agent, like the CPA, has ethical
and educational requirements to uphold.

Only CPAs, Enrolled Agents and Attorneys are allowed to practice and
fully represent clients before the IRS. In audit situations the difference in
these designations can be crucial. CPAs now have a limited attorney-client
privilege.

The best place to start your search for a tax professional is with a re-
ferral from a colleague. Ask who your friends are using and if they like that
person, and why. You can also check with your state society of CPAs or
with professional organizations such as Equity, SAG, ASCAP, ASJA,
AFM, etc. They will often have referrals available. When you get the name
of a few folks, decide who you want to talk to and make an appointment
with each for a free consultation. I would not hire any professional if that
person will not grant free consultation time. Try to interview several tax
advisors before you decide.

You will probably ask first if the accountant has experience with and
clients in your particular artistic endeavor. This is the most important question, and it will lead into a conversation that will let you know if this person
"gets it." Feel free to ask for references. Bring along some specific questions
about *your* return to ask; this allows you to really kick the tires. If you bring
along a copy of your past year's return, you can ask the accountant to quickly
review it and see if he or she has anything of interest to say about it. This is a
great way to see if the accountant spots some missed deductions or comes up
with some tax planning ideas.

I hate the question "What can you do for me?" and I'm sure I'm not
alone. It's better to ask specific questions, such as:

✓ "Reviewing my returns from last year do you think I missed any
      deductions?"
✓ "Do my deductions from last year seem reasonable?"
✓ "Do you see any audit flags?"
✓ "Reviewing last year's return, do you have any ideas on how I
      could reduce my taxes this year?"
✓ "Do you consider tax planning a part of the preparation process?"
✓ "Are you available for questions during the year and do you charge
      extra for this service?"
✓ "Do you have a Website?"
✓ "Do you have other clients that are in my profession and do you
      enjoy working with them?"

✓ "How do you bill, and when do you get paid?"
✓ "Approximately how much will it cost for you to prepare my tax return?"
✓ "I often have other states to file in. Are you familiar with tax returns from other states?"
✓ "How do you help clients that get audited?"
✓ "Have you ever read any of the IRS MSSP audit guides?"
✓ "Do you have checklists or other worksheets that will help me prepare my information for you?"
✓ "Will you be preparing my return personally?"
✓ "Do you make it a practice to sit with your clients and review the information before you prepare the return?"
✓ "How early should I make an appointment with you?"
✓ "How long does it usually take you to complete the return?"
✓ "Can I communicate with you directly via e-mail to make an appointment or to ask questions?"

When you finish an interview like this you will know if you have any rapport with the accountant (part of my second important *"C"*—communication). If you don't feel comfortable talking with your accountant, you won't be inclined to ask questions. When you do not ask questions, you will not get the best result on your tax return. It is through conversing with my clients that I have found we really ferret out all the deductions. Checklists are great but they only go so far.

A final reminder: Even though you have someone else prepare your return, you are the person ultimately responsible for the information on it. There is a statement on your 1040 tax return printed over the place where you sign that reads: "Under penalties of perjury, I declare that I have examined this return, and accompanying schedules and statements, and to the best of my knowledge and belief they are true, correct and complete."

10

Tax Planning

Due to the changing nature of tax law, I am not going to mention many specifics of tax planning. I will be posting weekly tax tips and other up to date information on the book's Website, www.arts-taxinfo.com, so be sure to visit there before deciding on any of the strategies discussed here.

Tax planning should be a vital part of your work with your tax advisor and should accomplish two things:

1. Lower your tax liability
2. Remove any surprises from the tax liability you do have

By being proactive in developing tax strategies with your advisor, you will make changes in your business that will lower your tax liability. Your tax advisor will be able to estimate your liability so that you can plan your cash flow properly and not have any nasty surprises at year-end.

Tax planning has two main goals:

1. Delaying taxes
2. Lowering taxes

While most tax planning concerns delaying the payment of income taxes, there are some schemes that actually lower the tax you pay. Some strategies do both.

The very heart of this book has been essentially a tax planning exercise. By being aware of your income and expenses you find how to maximize your deductions and lower your taxes. When you understand your tax situation, you are much better prepared to strategize and be proactive with your finances.

Timing Your Deductions

The basic technique in tax planning concerns the timing of deductions. I have touched on this throughout the book, as when I talked about purchasing equipment or moving deductions into the current year by spending money (or charging expenses) in December. This accelerates the expense into the current year. Now if the current year is a low-income year and you expect higher income next year, you may prefer not to do this. In that case it may be better for you to push the deduction forward into next year, and offset it against higher income and higher tax brackets. A decision such as this is an essential part of the important year-end meeting with your tax advisor. Work with your advisor to decide when major expenses should take place. You do need to have a good grasp of your finances and expected income first.

If the expense is the purchase of a computer, camera, musical instrument or some other asset you have the option of using the Section 179 election, an election that allows you to write-off the purchase of up to $24,000 (adjusted annually) in equipment or other personal property in 2001. This can be a tremendous late in the year tax saving move, especially when you are surprised at year-end with more income than you were expecting.

I always enjoy questions that begin with "Should I buy . . . ?" Let's be clear, NEVER buy anything, anytime simply to save taxes. So I respond to the above questions, "Well do you need (whatever the expense or asset is)?" When I discuss spending money in December, I am talking about an expense or purchase that is definitely going to be made within the first two or three months of the next year. We are just considering whether to move it into the current year.

Artists tend to overlook what I call "cross-over" expenses. They must not forget personal assets that have been used in the production of income. Frequently expenses are not an "all or nothing" proposition. As we have already said, deductions such as Internet service, home office and cars, are going to be allocated with some costs to your business and the balance to personal use.

Certain expenses are deductible only to the extent they exceed set income "floors." You will recall that the Form 2106 used to deduct employee business expenses must exceed 2% of your adjusted gross income. If you find you are close to these income floors, try to bunch payment of as many expenses into one tax year as possible to secure your deduction.

For 2001, the deduction for the health insurance expenses of self-employed individuals and their spouses and dependents is 60% of the cost of the policy; it will stay at this rate until tax year 2002 when it moves up again. This is a deduction very much subject to change in pending tax legislation, so check www.arts-taxinfo.com for the latest information.

Retirement Planning

You can set up a retirement plan if you are self-employed or have self-employment income such as royalties or other non-W-2 contract income. These plans allow you to start building a tax-deferred retirement fund and help to reduce current taxes in the process. Any funds you put into the plan are fully tax deductible for federal purposes (and sometimes for state purposes) and the earnings within the plan are not taxed until the money is taken out.

Simplified Employee Pensions (SEPs) – The SEP is the most common retirement plan for self-employed individuals. The maximum deduction allowed contribution to a SEP is 13.0435% of compensation up to $25,500 (in 2001). Compensation for the self-employed individual is calculated as the net Schedule C income less the self-employment tax deduction from page one of the 1040.

Keogh/Profit Sharing Plans – Keogh/Profit Sharing plans offer self-employed individuals an excellent way to set aside money for retirement. These plans must cover any eligible employees you may have. Contributions to the plan (within tax law limits) and any earnings on plan investments are not taxed until distributed from the plan. Keogh plans may be either defined contribution or defined benefit plans. Defined contribution plans provide for employer contributions to individual plan accounts for employees (and the self-employed owner). Defined benefit plans don't maintain individual accounts. Instead, the employer funds the plan based on projections of how much the plan will need to pay promised retirement benefits.

The above two retirement plans should be established by year-end, although tax-deductible contributions can be made anytime up until the return is timely filed (with extensions this can be delayed up to October 15 of the following year).

Note: If you're close to retirement age, you may be able to build a retirement fund more quickly with a defined benefit than with a defined contribution plan.

SIMPLE Retirement Plans - Self-employed individuals and small-business owners have a newer type of plan available to them. A "saving incentive match plan for employees" or "SIMPLE" retirement plan may be structured either as an Individual Retirement Account (IRA) for each employee or as a 401(K) salary deferral plan. Employers currently without a plan and employing 100 or fewer employees earning at least $5,000 each in compensation during the previous year are eligible to adopt a SIMPLE retirement plan. In a SIMPLE Individual Retirement Account, employees (and self-employed persons) can elect to contribute up to $6,500 in 2001 to the plan (adjusted annually for inflation). The employer generally must match employee elective contributions dollar-for-dollar up to 3% of the employee's compensation. However, a lower match may be elected in no more than two of any five years. Contributions are deductible by the employer and excludable from the employee's income.

IRAs are always an option if you already have a retirement plan available, but wish to put away some additional funds. You may contribute up to $2,000 annually in 2001 an IRA account (moving up to $3,000 in the tax year 2002). The deductibility of your contribution is dependent on several factors: (1) your level of earned income (2) whether you or your spouse is eligible for an employer sponsored retirement plan and (3) your adjusted gross income. If you and your spouse are not eligible for an employers sponsored plan your entire allowable IRA contribution ($4,000 = $2,000 each) is deductible. If you and/or your spouse are able to participate in a plan, your deduction may be limited or eliminated altogether when your adjusted gross incomes exceed specific levels. Please check www.arts-taxinfo.com for the latest phase out amounts concerning IRA deductions.

Many of you have no doubt read about ROTH IRAs. The Roth IRA is an IRA account to which individuals may make nondeductible contributions of up to $2,000, (No more than $2,000 per year may be contributed *to all* IRAs maintained by an individual.) Distributions from Roth IRAs are generally federal and state tax free as long as they are made more than five tax years after the first tax year for which a contribution is made, and are made on or after the date on which the taxpayer turns 59-1/2.

This has been just a quick overview of some of the more common techniques and strategies employed in tax planning. You should always discuss any change with a qualified tax advisor who is familiar with your financial situation before making any decision. I would also caution you not to look at your work with your tax advisor as being a simple function of getting your tax return prepared at year-end. Make your work with him or her an ongoing process that balances planning and preparation.

11

In Closing

My goal in writing this book was to give you an understanding of the basic elements of your tax return especially your professional income and deductions. It was never intended to be comprehensive and should not be taken that way. Federal and state taxation is complicated and very much subject to interpretation. Your personal circumstances can weigh in heavily on whether a particular expense is deductible or not.

I hope that by reading this volume you walk away with enough of a feel for taxation that you will be ready to be proactive in organizing, planning and discussing your personal situation intelligently with your tax professional. I also hope that you will get your record keeping in order and be ready for an audit, should it come about. Above all, I hope you will NEVER forget any deductions and NEVER pay a dollar more in taxes than you have to!

While we have covered much ground, some things were beyond our scope such as the very complicated subject of foreign earnings, which changes depending on the country involved. I have only slightly addressed the matter of state taxation; many states follow federal law closely, but not all.

Tax laws, of course, are affected by the whimsy of our government, and because of this most of the issues I have discussed in this book are subject to change. I have tried to keep to the general matters that are unlikely to alter a lot, but some things will invariably change. To help you keep current with changes between updates of the book I will be posting information on the books website www.arts-taxinfo.com.

Lastly, I welcome your comments concerning the book. Let me know what you would change, or like to see added in subsequent editions. You may contact me through the book's website or directly via e-mail at priley@cpa-services.com. As my noble predecessor R. Brendan Hanlon said, I want to "keep this the best book of its kind on the market." With your help I think I can.

Appendix I
IRS Publications and Other Resources

These are some of the publications that are available free from IRS. You can call the IRS and order them or download them directly from the IRS Website: www.irs.gov

- Publication 334   Tax Guide for Small Business
- Publication 17   Your Federal Income Tax Guide
- Publication 463   Travel, Entertainment, Gift, and Car Expenses
- Publication 525   Taxable and Nontaxable Income
- Publication 529   Miscellaneous Deductions
- Publication 536   Net Operating Losses for Individuals, Estates, and Trusts
- Publication 538   Accounting Periods and Methods
- Publication 547   Casualties, Disasters, and Thefts
- Publication 587   Business Use of Your Home
- Publication 925   Passive Activity and At-Risk Rules
- Publication 936   Home Mortgage Interest Deduction
- Publication 946   How To Depreciate Property
- Publication 535   Business Expenses
- Publication 1542   Per Diem Rates
- Publication 917   Business Use of Your Car
- Publication 526   Charitable Contributions
- Publication 556   Examination of Returns, Appeal Rights and Refund Claims
- Publication 501   Exemptions and Standard Deductions
- Publication 910   Guide to Free Tax Services
- Publication 521   Moving Expenses
- Publication 560   Self-employed Retirement Plans
- Publication 533   Self-employment Tax

- Publication 54   Guide to US Citizens and Resident
                     Aliens Abroad
- Publication 505   Tax Withholding and Estimated Tax
- Publication 929   Tax Rules for Children and Dependents
- Publication 523   Tax Information on Selling your Home
- Publication 514   Foreign Tax Credit for Individuals
- Publication 530   Tax Information for First Time Home Owners
- Publication 552   Recordkeeping for Individuals
- Publication 531   Reporting Tip Income
- Publication 593   Tax Highlights for US Citizens and
                     Residents Going Abroad
- Publication 970   Tax Benefits for Higher Education

Other books you may wish to look at:

- *J.K. Lasser's* ™ *"Your Income Tax"* published annually by John Wiley & Sons, Inc. In my opinion the best overall, single income tax guide available.
- *What the IRS Doesn't Want You to Know* by Martin Kaplan, CPA, and Naomi Weiss, published by Villard Books. A great common sense book giving insight into the operations and quirks of the IRS. Essential reading if you are audited!
- *422 Tax Deductions for Businesses & Self-Employed Individuals* by Bernard B. Kamoroff, CPA, published by Bell Springs Publishing. Mr. Kamoroff is the first person that I have run across who attempts an alphabetical encyclopedia of tax deductions. Excellent and amazingly easy to read
- *Taxation of the Entertainment Industry* by Schuyler M. Moore, Esq., published by Panel Publications. The most comprehensive and professional book on the market.
- *U.S. Master Tax Guide* published by CCH Inc. This is the bible of the tax preparation industry, published annually and used by tax professionals the world over. CCH also publishes the excellent *State Tax Guide* annually, which is a superb quick reference to taxation state by state. These are beyond the needs of most laymen but may serve as an excellent reference to have on your shelf.

Appendix II
Automobile Mileage Between Cities

FROM / TO	Albany, N. Y.	Atlanta—Ga.	Baltimore, Md.	Boston, Mass.	Buffalo, N. Y.	Chicago, Ill.	Cincinnati, Ohio	Cleveland, Ohio	Columbus, Ohio	Dallas, Tex.	Denver, Colo.	Detroit, Mich.	Houston, Tex.	Indianapolis, Ind.	Kansas City, Mo.
Albany, N. Y.	.....	1068	*331*	*171*	*278*	*803*	*701*	*462*	*603*	1717	1835	*530*	1829	*757*	1278
Amarillo, Tex.	1817	1150	1669	1983	1501	1098	1136	1333	1207	362	438	1305	605	1033	583
Asheville, N. C.	890	230	504	*900*	755	647	359	585	437	999	1539	608	1061	464	902
Atlanta, Ga.	1068	.....	687	1083	914	707	472	726	580	814	1495	734	848	554	844
Baltimore, Md.	*331*	687	.....	*399*	353	*685*	502	*351*	*395*	1436	1617	*511*	1521	568	1062
Birmingham, Ala.	1223	155	842	1228	939	667	497	751	605	659	1376	759	713	507	738
Bismarck, N. D.	*1694*	1586	1563	1873	1403	866	1153	1215	1171	1196	793	1153	1470	1042	816
Boise, Idaho	2648	2288	2426	2807	2337	1820	1970	2149	2119	1684	884	1987	1877	1860	1444
Boston, Mass.	*171*	1083	399	.....	*447*	*972*	*882*	*631*	*772*	1837	2021	*699*	1928	*926*	1444
Buffalo, N. Y.	*278*	914	353	*447*	.....	*527*	*425*	*186*	*327*	1421	1551	252	1533	*481*	984
Calgary, Alta.	2555	2496	2404	2714	2280	1727	2008	2056	2026	1916	1116	1994	2159	1917	1645
Charleston, W. Va.	*683*	529	406	*795*	457	488	211	268	174	1111	1434	362	1238	321	790
Chattanooga, Tenn.	1052	120	660	1085	791	589	349	603	457	799	1368	611	861	434	731
Cheyenne, Wyo.	1817	1525	1663	1962	1492	975	1207	1318	1271	903	103	1242	1146	1097	694
Chicago, Ill.	*803*	707	*685*	*972*	*527*	.....	324	*341*	359	957	1034	*293*	1110	184	507
Cincinnati, Ohio	*701*	472	502	*882*	*425*	324	.....	239	106	960	1161	255	1102	109	601
Cleveland, Ohio	*462*	726	*351*	*631*	*186*	*341*	239	.....	141	1233	1363	*167*	1356	295	794
Colorado Spgs, Colo.	1875	1463	1672	2088	1583	1095	1213	1395	1282	731	69	1382	974	1106	612
Columbia, S. C.	854	218	512	903	852	811	565	664	538	1032	1695	781	1102	637	1058
Columbus, Ohio	*603*	580	*395*	*772*	*327*	359	106	141	.....	1068	1225	185	1210	173	670
Dallas, Tex.	1717	814	1436	1837	1421	957	960	1233	1068	.....	800	1200	243	933	521
Denver, Colo.	1835	1495	1617	2021	1551	1034	1161	1363	1225	800	.....	1321	1043	1051	644
Des Moines, Ia.	1152	945	1038	1331	881	344	578	673	664	736	691	611	973	468	209
Detroit, Mich.	*530*	734	*511*	*699*	252	*293*	255	*167*	185	1200	1321	.....	1307	277	766
Duluth, Minn.	1324	1203	1193	1503	974	496	797	847	815	1147	1072	756	1428	686	620
El Paso, Tex.	2237	1441	2063	2400	1941	1515	1556	1753	1627	627	721	1725	750	1453	1000
Evansville, Ind.	998	413	769	*1104*	678	297	236	490	344	764	1075	436	881	164	431
Fargo, N. D.	1498	1390	1367	1677	1207	670	957	1019	975	1136	955	957	1379	846	669
Ft. Smith, Ark.	1422	696	1272	1602	1126	710	741	938	849	295	815	910	497	638	309
Ft. Wayne, Ind.	*674*	*667*	*556*	*843*	*398*	175	151	*212*	154	1046	1161	161	1148	116	607
Galveston, Tex.	1877	896	1550	1957	1592	1160	1150	1404	1258	293	1093	1355	50	1007	814
Great Falls, Mont.	2366	2174	2235	2525	1981	1538	1809	1867	1837	1556	756	1805	1799	1699	1323
Greensboro, N. C.	*675*	352	320	716	688	786	*479*	536	*442*	1166	1686	630	1254	*589*	1042
Harrisburg, Pa.	*338*	762	74	*398*	284	*655*	*484*	*321*	*382*	1469	1695	*481*	1582	*556*	1046
Hartford, Conn.	*109*	1011	*301*	104	*393*	*918*	*784*	577	*682*	1736	1974	*645*	1827	*863*	1357
Helena, Mont.	2379	2197	2246	2536	2066	1549	1832	1878	1846	1612	812	1826	1855	1722	1346
Houston, Tex.	1829	868	1521	1928	1533	1110	1102	1356	1210	243	1043	1307	.....	1035	764
Indianapolis, Ind.	*757*	554	568	*926*	*481*	184	109	295	173	933	1051	277	1035	.....	494
Jacksonville, Fla.	1165	324	799	1198	1187	1036	796	962	875	1024	1789	1063	958	881	1175
Kansas City, Mo.	1278	844	1062	1444	984	507	601	794	670	521	644	766	764	494	.....
Knoxville, Tenn.	911	192	548	944	722	568	280	534	388	890	1427	542	973	373	790
Las Vegas, Nev.	2756	2024	2519	2915	2424	1887	2010	2236	2225	1251	914	2174	1501	1951	1457
Lexington, Ky.	*875*	387	598	*987*	527	372	85	339	193	919	1242	347	1036	188	*598*
Lincoln, Neb.	1369	1076	1197	1535	1058	548	741	882	805	640	493	809	883	631	225
Little Rock, Ark.	1403	542	1101	1502	1081	661	665	893	756	335	967	865	452	·593	408
Los Angeles, Cal.	2941	2257	2793	3107	2645	2175	2260	2457	2331	1443	1265	2429	1566	2157	1728
Louisville, Ky.	*870*	440	641	*976*	550	305	108	362	216	852	1168	370	994	114	524
Memphis, Tenn.	1273	403	962	1363	953	549	511	744	619	474	1103	716	591	444	466

Italics denote shortest routes using one or more turnpikes

FROM / TO	Los Angeles, Cal.	Louisville, Ky.	Memphis, Tenn.	Miami, Fla.	Minneapolis-St. Paul	New Orleans, La.	New York, N. Y.	Omaha, Neb.	Philadelphia, Pa.	Richmond, Va.	St. Louis, Mo.	Salt Lake City, Utah	San Francisco, Cal.	Seattle, Wash.	Washington, D. C.
Albany, N. Y.	2941	846	1273	1470	1242	1592	169	1310	236	507	1070	2276	3008	2979	369
Amarillo, Tex.	1124	1059	747	1736	1042	869	1789	678	1699	1616	792	899	1457	1789	1630
Asheville, N. C.	2396	371	525	773	1062	706	696	1054	604	383	638	2042	2729	2814	469
Atlanta, Ga.	2257	440	403	681	1122	524	875	1056	783	561	587	1991	2644	2773	648
Baltimore, Md.	2793	641	962	1159	1112	1211	187	1156	97	144	806	2122	2881	2849	38
Birmingham, Ala.	2102	394	244	796	1079	357	1030	950	938	719	548	1864	2440	2678	769
Bismarck, N. D.	1740	1156	1299	2267	437	1684	1720	604	1623	1654	999	1000	1759	1263	1559
Boise, Idaho	900	1968	1934	2993	1477	2141	2646	1270	2557	2492	1701	373	653	510	2506
Boston, Mass.	3107	976	1363	1550	1422	1609	216	1469	304	540	1239	2424	3187	3125	437
Buffalo, N. Y.	2645	550	953	1450	952	1296	445	999	366	512	797	1954	2717	2687	361
Calgary, Alta.	1624	2195	2135	3157	1329	2375	2553	1493	2464	2638	1889	889	1479	760	2400
Charleston, W. Va.	2449	266	647	1046	903	936	587	911	497	311	533	1877	2636	2656	367
Chattanooga, Tenn.	2196	320	325	801	1019	505	848	936	756	545	467	1871	2529	2653	621
Cheyenne, Wyo.	1194	1205	1231	2213	840	1400	1844	507	1750	1729	938	461	1218	1300	1740
Chicago, Ill.	2175	305	549	1388	415	941	841	482	760	788	294	1437	2200	2172	685
Cincinnati, Ohio	2260	108	511	1132	716	854	653	700	572	622	340	1666	2425	2435	492
Cleveland, Ohio	2457	362	744	1314	764	1108	507	811	426	479	611	1766	2529	2501	351
Colorado Spgs., Colo.	1172	1136	1018	2102	975	1238	1895	580	1768	1713	869	580	1339	1371	1671
Columbia, S. C.	2495	544	649	650	1227	724	700	1227	603	363	794	2198	2882	2980	468
Columbus, Ohio	2331	216	619	1210	734	962	551	764	470	485	411	1730	2492	2471	395
Dallas, Tex.	1443	852	474	1350	991	507	1629	679	1537	1341	641	1250	1800	2151	1402
Denver, Colo.	1265	1168	1103	2143	916	1297	1807	552	1712	1745	901	530	1270	1381	1614
Des Moines, Ia.	1840	625	620	1626	255	1023	1189	139	1086	1122	358	1105	1864	1844	1035
Detroit, Mich.	2429	370	716	1374	702	1116	667	750	586	650	560	1704	2467	2439	511
Duluth, Minn.	2174	800	977	1884	156	1377	1342	520	1253	1284	676	1439	2198	1713	1189
El Paso, Tex.	816	1476	1101	2001	1459	1135	2175	1095	2100	1968	1212	898	1241	1785	2029
Evansville, Ind.	2090	128	280	1085	712	683	918	643	828	705	174	1571	2330	2353	732
Fargo, N. D.	1925	960	1103	2058	241	1504	1516	457	1427	1458	803	1190	1949	1459	1363
Ft. Smith, Ark.	1581	664	290	1330	773	576	1394	521	1304	1159	397	1326	1914	2140	1233
Ft. Wayne, Ind.	2270	220	557	1340	576	960	712	646	631	639	354	1612	2371	2313	556
Galveston, Tex.	1616	1042	639	1316	1278	372	1749	972	1646	1435	861	1554	2041	2395	1468
Great Falls, Mont.	1323	1873	1811	2835	1007	2053	2384	1171	2275	2316	1567	588	1292	706	2231
Greensboro, N. C.	2584	618	713	837	1201	876	508	1179	416	230	785	2230	2947	2964	281
Harrisburg, Pa.	2740	598	995	1237	1072	1185	186	1143	105	219	794	2074	2833	2809	112
Hartford, Conn.	3020	897	1262	1490	1354	1472	118	1444	206	439	1185	2356	3119	3082	339
Helena, Mont.	1229	1894	1834	2871	1030	2007	2415	1192	2286	2317	1603	494	1128	617	2242
Houston, Tex.	1566	994	591	1300	1228	385	1675	922	1572	1406	813	1504	1991	2394	1482
Indianapolis, Ind.	2157	114	444	1235	605	847	724	590	643	632	238	1556	2315	2250	568
Jacksonville, Fla.	2467	764	671	356	1473	573	1031	1373	898	658	911	2287	2869	3101	763
Kansas City, Mo.	1728	524	466	1516	464	868	1220	212	1160	1101	257	1174	1899	1994	1059
Knoxville, Tenn.	2287	259	415	871	983	617	736	985	644	433	526	1930	2620	2712	509
Las Vegas, Nev.	289	1933	1621	2625	1729	1758	2707	1466	2617	2490	1666	446	596	1195	2504
Lexington, Ky.	2257	74	445	1068	787	769	779	810	681	503	341	1738	2497	2520	559
Lincoln, Neb.	1663	749	715	1757	423	1093	1369	59	1265	1263	482	928	1687	1697	1194
Little Rock, Ark.	1735	524	139	1176	836	460	1294	620	1198	1008	361	1478	2068	2294	1067
Los Angeles, Cal.	....	2183	1871	2817	2018	1951	2913	1701	2823	2740	1916	735	408	1190	2754
Louisville, Ky.	2138	....	385	1121	720	751	790	704	700	577	267	1664	2423	2446	604
Memphis, Tenn.	1871	385	....	1030	863	403	1155	680	1059	869	301	1616	2204	2430	928

TO \ FROM	Albany, N. Y.	Atlanta—Ga.	Baltimore, Md.	Boston, Mass.	Buffalo, N. Y.	Chicago, Ill.	Cincinnati, Ohio	Cleveland, Ohio	Columbus, Ohio	Dallas, Tex.	Denver, Colo.	Detroit, Mich.	Houston, Tex.	Indianapolis, Ind.	Kansas City, Mo.
Miami, Fla.	1470	681	1159	1550	1450	1388	1132	1314	1210	1350	2143	1374	1300	1235	1516
Milwaukee, Wis.	891	796	773	1060	615	91	429	429	447	1046	1050	381	1199	279	596
Minneapolis-St. Paul.	1242	1122	1112	1422	952	415	716	764	734	991	916	702	1228	605	464
Mobile, Ala.	1433	365	1052	1448	1218	870	742	1030	850	599	1389	1038	537	748	853
Montgomery, Ala.	1245	177	864	1260	1030	767	588	842	696	659	1459	850	725	605	835
Montreal, Que.	228	1267	580	327	409	886	851	597	743	1808	1914	593	1900	855	1359
Nashville, Tenn.	1104	257	742	1138	775	451	291	587	399	694	1231	553	811	297	587
New Orleans, La.	1592	524	1211	1609	1296	941	854	1108	962	507	1297	1116	385	847	868
New York, N. Y.	169	875	187	216	445	841	653	507	551	1629	1807	667	1675	724	1220
Oklahoma City, Okla.	1555	888	1407	1721	1239	826	876	1071	945	211	618	1043	454	771	358
Omaha, Neb.	1310	1056	1156	1469	999	482	700	811	764	679	552	750	922	590	212
Philadelphia, Pa.	236	783	97	304	366	760	572	426	470	1537	1712	586	1572	643	1160
Phoenix, Ariz.	2525	1839	2405	2717	2255	1793	1872	2067	1941	1040	827	2013	1163	1767	1276
Pittsburgh, Pa.	492	752	230	598	220	459	284	125	182	1247	1410	285	1389	356	853
Portland, Me.	238	1188	501	105	530	1053	972	722	900	1942	2073	782	2067	1022	1516
Portland, Ore.	3073	2803	2935	3252	2768	2265	2478	2594	2564	2137	1337	2532	2385	2368	1952
Providence, R. I.	166	1083	366	43	450	975	849	634	747	1808	2056	801	1899	921	1429
Quebec, Que.	401	1440	753	402	582	1053	1024	743	884	1981	2087	766	2073	1028	1532
Raleigh, N. C.	645	402	303	699	671	866	559	616	522	1216	1766	710	1304	669	1122
Rapid City, S. D.	1770	1592	1619	1929	1459	942	1252	1271	1241	1134	406	1209	1402	1137	761
Richmond, Va.	507	561	144	540	512	788	522	479	485	1341	1745	650	1406	632	1101
Sacramento, Cal.	2919	2614	2792	3096	2626	2109	2336	2438	2403	1815	1181	2376	1961	2226	1810
St. Joseph, Mo.	1274	905	1056	1440	978	500	600	790	664	581	561	767	818	490	54
St. Louis, Mo.	1070	587	806	1239	797	294	340	611	411	641	901	560	813	238	257
Salt Lake City, Utah.	2276	1991	2122	2424	1954	1437	1666	1766	1730	1250	530	1704	1504	1556	1174
San Antonio, Tex.	2012	1098	1706	2104	1692	1251	1250	1504	1358	274	954	1474	196	1183	795
San Diego, Cal.	2912	2184	2768	3082	2620	2191	2235	2432	2306	1370	1192	2378	1493	2132	1682
San Francisco, Cal.	3008	2644	2881	3187	2717	2200	2425	2529	2492	1800	1270	2467	1991	2315	1899
Santa Fe, N. M.	2110	1430	1959	2276	1801	1378	1428	1613	1487	642	391	1585	885	1313	832
Sault Ste. Marie.	775	1074	899	940	553	491	604	513	530	1406	1453	352	1540	520	936
Scranton, Pa.	175	884	219	310	248	777	564	369	462	1570	1761	500	1712	635	1166
Seattle, Wash.	2979	2773	2849	3125	2687	2172	2435	2501	2471	2151	1381	2439	2394	2250	1994
Shreveport, La.	1623	627	1312	1713	1303	890	862	1115	969	187	977	1066	241	794	565
Sioux City, Ia.	1318	1149	1207	1497	1027	510	782	839	819	785	613	777	1028	672	318
Sioux Falls, S. D.	1396	1237	1265	1555	1085	568	870	897	867	873	695	835	1116	760	406
Spokane, Wash.	2684	2478	2559	2863	2392	1882	2140	2211	2181	1837	1086	2149	2080	2072	1627
Springfield, Ill.	969	600	754	1138	696	193	301	510	365	795	863	459	906	192	306
Springfield, Mo.	1245	725	1077	1411	949	522	564	761	635	472	817	733	674	461	174
Syracuse, N. Y.	139	1014	327	309	153	685	595	344	490	1558	1704	405	1700	641	1137
Tampa, Fla.	1370	482	1010	1396	1378	1194	954	1160	1071	1101	1901	1216	1057	1036	1292
Toledo, Ohio.	572	678	454	741	296	239	198	110	128	1149	1254	57	1251	220	710
Toronto, Ont.	400	1014	468	570	100	542	500	288	426	1453	1559	238	1545	510	1004
Tulsa, Okla.	1444	830	1276	1610	1128	720	765	960	834	278	701	932	521	660	249
Vancouver, B. C.	3121	2890	2971	3300	2830	2313	2594	2642	2612	2294	1498	2561	2537	2484	2075
Washington, D. C.	369	648	38	437	361	685	492	351	395	1402	1614	511	1482	568	1059
Wichita, Kans.	1496	1014	1348	1662	1200	741	815	1012	868	385	515	964	628	712	198
Wilmington, N. C.	757	441	398	796	766	961	682	739	645	1255	1876	836	1305	792	1234
Winnipeg, Man.	1643	1584	1620	1808	1421	877	1178	1226	1196	1375	1105	1203	1618	1067	908

TO \ FROM	Los Angeles, Cal.	Louisville, Ky.	Memphis, Tenn.	Miami, Fla.	Minneapolis-St. Paul	New Orleans, La.	New York, N.Y.	Omaha, Neb.	Philadelphia, Pa.	Richmond, Va.	St. Louis, Mo.	Salt Lake City, Utah	San Francisco, Cal.	Seattle, Wash.	Washington, D.C.
Miami, Fla.	2817	1121	1030		1803	900	1350	1728	1247	1015	1259	2600	3219	3454	1123
Milwaukee, Wis.	2199	394	638	1477	337	1030	935	498	848	877	367	1465	2223	2055	773
Minneapolis-St. Paul	2018	719	863	1803		1263	1261	364	1172	1203	562	1283	2042	1642	1108
Mobile, Ala.	2042	634	373	775	1304	152	1240	1062	1148	926	642	1877	2444	2701	1013
Montgomery, Ala.	2102	491	345	730	1176	340	1052	1047	960	738	638	1961	2504	2775	825
Montreal, Que.	3022	959	1309	1742	1150	1602	392	1348	495	724	1106	2303	3060	2747	619
Nashville, Tenn.	2091	183	220	929	868	568	930	806	840	628	330	1734	2424	2516	703
New Orleans, La.	1951	751	403	900	1263		1365	1080	1261	1050	701	1808	2300	2658	1138
New York, N.Y.	2913	790	1155	1350	1261	1365		1300	92	332	962	2303	3062	2975	225
Oklahoma City, Okla.	1386	797	485	1525	852	679	1517	488	1437	1354	530	1106	1719	1920	1368
Omaha, Neb.	1701	704	680	1728	364	1080	1300		1243	1222	469	966	1725	1735	1155
Philadelphia, Pa.	2823	700	1059	1247	1172	1261	92	1225		240	885	2209	2968	2875	135
Phoenix, Ariz.	403	1793	1481	2414	1743	1548	2500	1349	2501	2350	1526	720	828	1535	2364
Pittsburgh, Pa.	2547	395	798	1258	874	1125	386	950	305	352	596	1916	2675	2611	230
Portland, Me.	3179	1080	1468	1696	1480	1714	313	1515	406	645	1263	2470	3233	3016	540
Portland, Ore.	1004	2489	2442	3482	1585	2634	3111	1778	3002	3000	2222	826	674	176	2931
Providence, R.I.	3092	969	1334	1562	1426	1544	183	1516	271	511	1242	2428	3183	3154	404
Quebec, Que.	3195	1132	1482	1915	1323	1775	565	1521	665	897	1295	2470	3233	2920	792
Raleigh, N.C.	2659	598	793	848	1281	926	491	1334	399	159	865	2310	2997	3044	264
Rapid City, S.D.	1421	1272	1251	2293	597	1630	1772	549	1679	1789	1005	686	1445	1197	1635
Richmond, Va.	2740	577	869	1015	1203	1050	332	1222	240		844	2198	2957	2940	105
Sacramento, Cal.	386	2334	2174	3189	1953	2322	2976	1636	2882	2868	2067	670	89	794	2789
St. Joseph, Mo.	1772	578	544	1586	436	922	1246	158	1156	1122	311	1072	1831	1866	1053
St. Louis, Mo.	1916	267	301	1259	562	701	962	469	885	844		1397	2156	2251	806
Salt Lake City, Utah	735	1664	1616	2600	1283	1808	2303	966	2191	2209	1397		759	889	2119
San Antonio, Tex.	1379	1142	739	1525	1259	581	1894	953	1798	1580	966	1426	1804	2305	1667
San Diego, Cal.	124	2158	1846	2744	2068	1878	2888	1714	2798	2715	1891	785	556	1304	2729
San Francisco, Cal.	408	2423	2204	3219	2042	2300	3062	1725	2968	2957	2156	759		850	2878
Santa Fe, N.M.	896	1339	1027	2016	1307	1149	2069	905	1992	1896	1072	625	1229	1514	1941
Sault Ste. Marie	2555	634	964	1753	537	1367	937	901	941	988	727	1820	2579	2134	887
Scranton, Pa.	2860	718	1112	1366	1162	1415	125	1229	122	341	873	2163	2922	2919	257
Seattle, Wash.	1190	2446	2430	3454	1642	2658	2975	1735	2875	2940	2251	889	850		2845
Shreveport, La.	1630	753	350	1187	1029	320	1505	777	1409	1191	572	1465	2032	2279	1241
Sioux City, Ia.	1714	829	808	1830	336	1186	1336	106	1247	1326	562	996	1755	1640	1203
Sioux Falls, S.D.	1752	917	896	1918	248	1274	1414	194	1325	1414	650	1053	1812	1555	1261
Spokane, Wash.	1261	2151	2135	3159	1347	2344	2708	1440	2619	2650	1884	756	939	295	2555
Springfield, Ill.	2034	280	404	1296	502	804	944	446	926	820	101	1374	2133	2238	751
Springfield, Mo.	1696	487	316	1391	602	694	1217	386	1127	1132	220	1314	2029	2096	1058
Syracuse, N.Y.	2798	703	1109	1489	1106	1349	301	1147	262	471	882	2102	2893	2840	366
Tampa, Fla.	2544	922	802	272	1633	672	1229	1504	1096	863	1068	2383	2946	3232	971
Toledo, Ohio	2373	314	660	1359	637	1060	610	704	529	590	506	1659	2422	2414	454
Toronto, Ont.	2667	608	954	1630	957	1354	527	1004	498	612	751	1957	2705	2587	507
Tulsa, Okla.	1497	686	427	1467	713	713	1416	401	1326	1331	419	1189	1830	2003	1257
Vancouver, B.C.	1364	2563	2447	3607	1759	2840	3144	1852	3031	3062	2296	1032	993	143	2967
Washington, D.C.	2754	602	928	1123	1108	1138	225	1155	135	105	806	2119	2878	2845	
Wichita, Kans.	1509	738	611	1659	678	853	1448	314	1358	1315	471	1003	1762	1817	1309
Wilmington, N.C.	2698	708	855	778	1376	927	580	1391	477	254	975	2379	3085	3156	359
Winnipeg, Man.	2120	1223	1343	2265	457	1746	1773	696	1670	1665	1042	1385	2144	1473	1571

Appendix III
Monthly Expense "Spread Sheets"

These "spread sheets" are intended to provide you with the means of doing some easy bookkeeping as the year goes on, thereby reducing the amount of work necessary to file your return at year's end. Those items with asterisks must be backed up by receipted evidence no matter how small.

The categorization is not arbitrary. For example, hotel or airport tips while you are travelling may be used to account for reported per diem but tips to dressers in your tax home may not.

Year ——— Month ——— Day	Out of Town Meals	Out of Town Lodging*	Out of Town Laundry & Cleaning	Out of Town Local Transport	Rental Car & Gas*	Business Mileage on Personal Car	Tolls and Parking*	Traveling Tips (Hotel, Air Porter)	Air, Rail for Business*
1									
2									
3									
4									
5									
6									
7									
8									
9									
10									
11									
12									
13									
14									
15									
16									
17									
18									
19									
20									
21									
22									
23									
24									
25									
26									
27									
28									
29									
30									
31									
Monthly TOTALS									

Local Transp. for Interviews, Auditions	Dresser, Doorman Tips	Trade Papers	Coin Phone for Business	Business Meals (Entertainment) (over $25*)	Other Deductible Local Transp.			Name of Location of out-of-town job	
									1
									2
									3
									4
									5
									6
									7
									8
									9
									10
									11
									12
									13
									14
									15
									16
									17
									18
									19
									20
									21
									22
									23
									24
									25
									26
									27
									28
									29
									30
									31

Year ___ Month ___ Day	Out of Town Meals	Out of Town Lodging*	Out of Town Laundry & Cleaning	Out of Town Local Transport	Rental Car & Gas*	Business Mileage on Personal Car	Tolls and Parking*	Traveling Tips (Hotel, Air Porter)	Air, Rail for Business*
1									
2									
3									
4									
5									
6									
7									
8									
9									
10									
11									
12									
13									
14									
15									
16									
17									
18									
19									
20									
21									
22									
23									
24									
25									
26									
27									
28									
29									
30									
31									
Monthly TOTALS									

Local Transp. for Interviews, Auditions	Dresser, Doorman Tips	Trade Papers	Coin Phone for Business	Business Meals (Entertainment) (over $25*)	Other Deductible Local Transp.			Name of Location of out-of-town job	
									1
									2
									3
									4
									5
									6
									7
									8
									9
									10
									11
									12
									13
									14
									15
									16
									17
									18
									19
									20
									21
									22
									23
									24
									25
									26
									27
									28
									29
									30
									31

Year ___ Month ___ Day	Out of Town Meals	Out of Town Lodging*	Out of Town Laundry & Cleaning	Out of Town Local Transport	Rental Car & Gas*	Business Mileage on Personal Car	Tolls and Parking*	Traveling Tips (Hotel, Air Porter)	Air, Rail for Business*
1									
2									
3									
4									
5									
6									
7									
8									
9									
10									
11									
12									
13									
14									
15									
16									
17									
18									
19									
20									
21									
22									
23									
24									
25									
26									
27									
28									
29									
30									
31									
Monthly TOTALS									

Local Transp. for Interviews, Auditions	Dresser, Doorman Tips	Trade Papers	Coin Phone for Business	Business Meals (Entertainment) (over $25*)	Other Deductible Local Transp.			Name of Location of out-of-town job	
									1
									2
									3
									4
									5
									6
									7
									8
									9
									10
									11
									12
									13
									14
									15
									16
									17
									18
									19
									20
									21
									22
									23
									24
									25
									26
									27
									28
									29
									30
									31

Year Month Day	Out of Town Meals	Out of Town Lodging*	Out of Town Laundry & Cleaning	Out of Town Local Transport	Rental Car & Gas*	Business Mileage on Personal Car	Tolls and Parking*	Traveling Tips (Hotel, Air Porter)	Air, Rail for Business*
1									
2									
3									
4									
5									
6									
7									
8									
9									
10									
11									
12									
13									
14									
15									
16									
17									
18									
19									
20									
21									
22									
23									
24									
25									
26									
27									
28									
29									
30									
31									
Monthly TOTALS									

Local Transp. for Interviews, Auditions	Dresser, Doorman Tips	Trade Papers	Coin Phone for Business	Business Meals (Entertainment) (over $25*)	Other Deductible Local Transp.			Name of Location of out-ot-town job	
									1
									2
									3
									4
									5
									6
									7
									8
									9
									10
									11
									12
									13
									14
									15
									16
									17
									18
									19
									20
									21
									22
									23
									24
									25
									26
									27
									28
									29
									30
									31

Year ___ Month ___ Day	Out of Town Meals	Out of Town Lodging*	Out of Town Laundry & Cleaning	Out of Town Local Transport	Rental Car & Gas*	Business Mileage on Personal Car	Tolls and Parking*	Traveling Tips (Hotel, Air Porter)	Air, Rail for Business*
1									
2									
3									
4									
5									
6									
7									
8									
9									
10									
11									
12									
13									
14									
15									
16									
17									
18									
19									
20									
21									
22									
23									
24									
25									
26									
27									
28									
29									
30									
31									
Monthly **TOTALS**									

Local Transp. for Interviews, Auditions	Dresser, Doorman Tips	Trade Papers	Coin Phone for Business	Business Meals (Entertainment) (over $25*)	Other Deductible Local Transp.			Name of Location of out-of-town job	
									1
									2
									3
									4
									5
									6
									7
									8
									9
									10
									11
									12
									13
									14
									15
									16
									17
									18
									19
									20
									21
									22
									23
									24
									25
									26
									27
									28
									29
									30
									31

Year Month Day	Out of Town Meals	Out of Town Lodging*	Out of Town Laundry & Cleaning	Out of Town Local Transport	Rental Car & Gas*	Business Mileage on Personal Car	Tolls and Parking*	Traveling Tips (Hotel, Air Porter)	Air, Rail for Business*	
1										
2										
3										
4										
5										
6										
7										
8										
9										
10										
11										
12										
13										
14										
15										
16										
17										
18										
19										
20										
21										
22										
23										
24										
25										
26										
27										
28										
29										
30										
31										
Monthly TOTALS										

Local Transp. for Interviews, Auditions	Dresser, Doorman Tips	Trade Papers	Coin Phone for Business	Business Meals (Entertainment) (over $25*)	Other Deductible Local Transp.			Name of Location of out-ot-town job	
									1
									2
									3
									4
									5
									6
									7
									8
									9
									10
									11
									12
									13
									14
									15
									16
									17
									18
									19
									20
									21
									22
									23
									24
									25
									26
									27
									28
									29
									30
									31

Year Month Day	Out of Town Meals	Out of Town Lodging*	Out of Town Laundry & Cleaning	Out of Town Local Transport	Rental Car & Gas*	Business Mileage on Personal Car	Tolls and Parking*	Traveling Tips (Hotel, Air Porter)	Air, Rail for Business*
1									
2									
3									
4									
5									
6									
7									
8									
9									
10									
11									
12									
13									
14									
15									
16									
17									
18									
19									
20									
21									
22									
23									
24									
25									
26									
27									
28									
29									
30									
31									
Monthly **TOTALS**									

Local Transp. for Interviews, Auditions	Dresser, Doorman Tips	Trade Papers	Coin Phone for Business	Business Meals (Entertainment) (over $25*)	Other Deductible Local Transp.			Name of Location of out-ot-town job	
									1
									2
									3
									4
									5
									6
									7
									8
									9
									10
									11
									12
									13
									14
									15
									16
									17
									18
									19
									20
									21
									22
									23
									24
									25
									26
									27
									28
									29
									30
									31

Year ___ Month ___ Day	Out of Town Meals	Out of Town Lodging*	Out of Town Laundry & Cleaning	Out of Town Local Transport	Rental Car & Gas*	Business Mileage on Personal Car	Tolls and Parking*	Traveling Tips (Hotel, Air Porter)	Air, Rail for Business*
1									
2									
3									
4									
5									
6									
7									
8									
9									
10									
11									
12									
13									
14									
15									
16									
17									
18									
19									
20									
21									
22									
23									
24									
25									
26									
27									
28									
29									
30									
31									
Monthly **TOTALS**									

Local Transp. for Interviews, Auditions	Dresser, Doorman Tips	Trade Papers	Coin Phone for Business	Business Meals (Entertainment) (over $25*)	Other Deductible Local Transp.			Name of Location of out-ot-town job	
									1
									2
									3
									4
									5
									6
									7
									8
									9
									10
									11
									12
									13
									14
									15
									16
									17
									18
									19
									20
									21
									22
									23
									24
									25
									26
									27
									28
									29
									30
									31

Year ___ Month ___ Day	Out of Town Meals	Out of Town Lodging*	Out of Town Laundry & Cleaning	Out of Town Local Transport	Rental Car & Gas*	Business Mileage on Personal Car	Tolls and Parking*	Traveling Tips (Hotel, Air Porter)	Air, Rail for Business*
1									
2									
3									
4									
5									
6									
7									
8									
9									
10									
11									
12									
13									
14									
15									
16									
17									
18									
19									
20									
21									
22									
23									
24									
25									
26									
27									
28									
29									
30									
31									
Monthly TOTALS									

Local Transp. for Interviews, Auditions	Dresser, Doorman Tips	Trade Papers	Coin Phone for Business	Business Meals (Entertainment) (over $25*)	Other Deductible Local Transp.			Name of Location of out-of-town job	
									1
									2
									3
									4
									5
									6
									7
									8
									9
									10
									11
									12
									13
									14
									15
									16
									17
									18
									19
									20
									21
									22
									23
									24
									25
									26
									27
									28
									29
									30
									31

Year ——— Month ——— Day	Out of Town Meals	Out of Town Lodging*	Out of Town Laundry & Cleaning	Out of Town Local Transport	Rental Car & Gas*	Business Mileage on Personal Car	Tolls and Parking*	Traveling Tips (Hotel, Air Porter)	Air, Rail for Business*
1									
2									
3									
4									
5									
6									
7									
8									
9									
10									
11									
12									
13									
14									
15									
16									
17									
18									
19									
20									
21									
22									
23									
24									
25									
26									
27									
28									
29									
30									
31									
Monthly TOTALS									

Local Transp. for Interviews, Auditions	Dresser, Doorman Tips	Trade Papers	Coin Phone for Business	Business Meals (Entertainment) (over $25°)	Other Deductible Local Transp.			Name of Location of out-ot-town job	
									1
									2
									3
									4
									5
									6
									7
									8
									9
									10
									11
									12
									13
									14
									15
									16
									17
									18
									19
									20
									21
									22
									23
									24
									25
									26
									27
									28
									29
									30
									31

Year ___ Month ___ Day	Out of Town Meals	Out of Town Lodging*	Out of Town Laundry & Cleaning	Out of Town Local Transport	Rental Car & Gas*	Business Mileage on Personal Car	Tolls and Parking*	Traveling Tips (Hotel, Air Porter,	Air, Rail for Business*
1									
2									
3									
4									
5									
6									
7									
8									
9									
10									
11									
12									
13									
14									
15									
16									
17									
18									
19									
20									
21									
22									
23									
24									
25									
26									
27									
28									
29									
30									
31									
Monthly TOTALS									

Local Transp. for Interviews, Auditions	Dresser, Doorman Tips	Trade Papers	Coin Phone for Business	Business Meals (Entertainment) (over $25*)	Other Deductible Local Transp.			Name of Location of out-of-town job	
									1
									2
									3
									4
									5
									6
									7
									8
									9
									10
									11
									12
									13
									14
									15
									16
									17
									18
									19
									20
									21
									22
									23
									24
									25
									26
									27
									28
									29
									30
									31

Year ___ Month ___ Day	Out of Town Meals	Out of Town Lodging*	Out of Town Laundry & Cleaning	Out of Town Local Transport	Rental Car & Gas*	Business Mileage on Personal Car	Tolls and Parking*	Traveling Tips (Hotel, Air Porter)	Air, Rail for Business*
1									
2									
3									
4									
5									
6									
7									
8									
9									
10									
11									
12									
13									
14									
15									
16									
17									
18									
19									
20									
21									
22									
23									
24									
25									
26									
27									
28									
29									
30									
31									
Monthly TOTALS									

Local Transp. for Interviews, Auditions	Dresser, Doorman Tips	Trade Papers	Coin Phone for Business	Business Meals (Entertainment) (over $25*)	Other Deductible Local Transp.			Name of Location of out-ot-town job	
									1
									2
									3
									4
									5
									6
									7
									8
									9
									10
									11
									12
									13
									14
									15
									16
									17
									18
									19
									20
									21
									22
									23
									24
									25
									26
									27
									28
									29
									30
									31

Appendix IV
Record of Exemptions Claimed

Job	Date W-4 Submitted	# of Exemptions	Amended Y or N?

Job	Date W-4 Submitted	# of Exemptions	Amended Y or N?

Job	Date W-4 Submitted	# of Exemptions	Amended Y or N?

Job	Date W-4 Submitted	# of Exemptions	Amended Y or N?

Job	Date W-4 Submitted	# of Exemptions	Amended Y or N?

About the Author

Author Peter Jason Riley, CPA (priley@cpa-services.com) is president of the firm Riley & Associates, P.C. in Newburyport, Massachusetts (www.cpa-services.com), which offers specialized, strategic tax planning and preparation to a worldwide client base.

Mr. Riley's undergraduate education was in liberal arts—English, music, philosophy and history—at Northeastern University in Boston. After working in the film industry for several years he resumed his education at Merrimack College in Andover, where he received a BS in accounting and business administration in May of 1992. In December of 1990 he passed the two-day I.R.S. Enrolled Agent's tax certification exam, and upon graduation from Merrimack College he passed the C.P.A. exam, both at the first sitting.

Mr. Riley's passion, outside of his business, is music. An amateur guitar player, he writes monthly reviews for the journal *The Undertoad* on a wide variety of music from folk and blues to jazz and rock. His articles have appeared in *Just Jazz Guitar, Metronome, Art Calendar, Boston Blues Society Journal* and *The Boston Phoenix*. He is also a regular speaker and lecturer on tax and business issues at Boston area colleges and organizations.